IRELAND'S ECONOMIC CRASH

IRELAND'S ECONOMIC CRASH

A Radical Agenda for Change

Kieran Allen

The Liffey Press

Published by
The Liffey Press
Ashbrook House, 10 Main Street
Raheny, Dublin 5, Ireland
www.theliffeypress.com

A catalogue record of this book is
available from the British Library.

ISBN 978-1-905785-68-1

Printed in the Republic of Ireland by Colour Books

CONTENTS

PREFACE

THIS BOOK IS WRITTEN AS AN INTERVENTION in a public debate. For the past few months, I have watched with growing dismay a new consensus being forged by the dominant groups in Irish society. At first hesitantly, but now with greater confidence, they advocate their radical solutions to the current economic depression. They start by guilt-tripping the population, implying that 'we' were all responsible for the crash. And as punishment, they urge wage cuts and reductions in the public services, as if Ireland did not already have inadequately funded hospitals or schools.

Sometimes it is not put as baldly as this. An Orwellian technical language is used to promote 'income corrections' and social welfare 'adjustments'. But the sheer blandness of expression stands in marked contrast to the real social suffering it brings. I have borrowed the term from the French sociologist, Pierre Bourdieu, who used it in his excellent book, *The Weight of the World*. Suffering is social when it does not result from purely individual actions or decisions but has immediate social roots. It is not confined to material deprivation, although that is growing considerably, but destroys hopes and ambitions that were previously thought possible to achieve.

It is utterly amazing to watch academics and politicians, who uncritically worshipped the culture of light regulation and gung-ho market economics in the Celtic Tiger era, continue on as they were before. Virtually none of them saw the crash coming, and while some predicted the end of the property bubble, none envisaged a great 1930s-style depression. Yet they casually avoid a great elephant that is lumbering around the room. The approach is to do anything but address the central issue: capitalism is failing on a global stage and the urgent question that faces us is what alternative can be found.

I have tried to advance a number of practical solutions but I readily acknowledge there is a certain ambiguity about this. The solutions advocated come up against limitations of a for-profit system which organises production around private greed rather than human need. But all the more reason, then, to question why we accept a system that brought about insane gambling and speculation.

I have drawn on the help of a number of people to make this book possible. Alistair Fraser is one of the best proponents of a clear language style that I know, and his assistance in a number of chapters has been invaluable. Sinead Kennedy made detailed comments and put me right on some key points. Nick Clifton told me that I should give up on the Socialist Worker stuff and join the mainstream. I disagree, but was glad to get his feedback. Margaret O'Regan cast a very sharp eye over the book while Kevin Wingfield gave some help with the tables. Kulwant Gill corrected some of the material, and told me not to be negative about all the negativities around me. I have tried. There are others who prefer to remain nameless.

Finally, it was a great pleasure to find an Irish publisher who agreed to produce this book in record time. I am very grateful to David Givens of The Liffey Press for his speed of response and for the huge effort put into making this book possible.

Kieran Allen

May 2009

INTRODUCTION

EUROPE IS AMAZED AT THE MEASURES Ireland is taking to deal with its economic crisis. This, at least, is what Brian Lenihan thought. Speaking to delegates at the Irish League of Credit Unions in April 2009 he said, 'The steps taken had impressed our partners in Europe, who are amazed at our capacity to take pain. In France you would have riots if you tried to do this.'[1] It was obviously a little boast but Lenihan wanted to show how chuffed he was. Perhaps he just needed to show there was at least something he could be proud of. The implication was that his government had the Irish population more under control than the rebellious French.

Tommy Hogan, a 61-year-old Waterford Crystal worker, has a different view. When he drives his car past his old factory, he sometimes feels like smashing right through it. Tommy left the plant in 2008, after spending forty-two years of his life working there. He started in 1966 as a young apprentice learning his trade as a skilled glass cutter. After eight years he became a master craftsman, leading a team of three glass cutters.

Each day the teams stood in a line, elbows leaning on a worktable, sometimes in water. The whirring sound of the cutting blade was often deafening and most workers wore ear muffs. It was tough, hard and physical work turning out some of the best glass ornaments in the world. They cut stemware, giftware and hollow ware as the large vases were known. Sometimes, they were called to work in the 'specials' department, to cut large ornaments for upper-class locations like Windsor Castle or West-minster Abbey. It was exhausting but well paid, with the prospect of a secure pension at the end of it.

Or so the workers thought. When Tommy Hogan retired, he expected a substantial lump sum and a steady income of €390 a week. He had originally been part of a non-contributory scheme which the company paid for, but after 1989 he paid 5 per cent of his salary to his pension.

On 30 January 2008, there was a bombshell announcement: Waterford Crystal was closing its Kilbarry plant and the company was going into liquidation. The company's pension scheme had been in difficulty for some time – owing to the vagaries of the stock markets – but the turbulence of recent years sent it careering into a large deficit. When this occurs, a specific procedure is put into operation. Normally, the pension fund is wound up and existing pensioners receive the first priority on payments. If more funds are available after that, they are divided up to make provision for existing workers who will only get a proportion of their original entitlements. In the case of Waterford Crystal, that proportion amounted to only 20 per cent.

Tommy Hogan was singularly unfortunate. He had left the factory on a 'deferred retirement package' and his pension payments had not fully kicked in – so he was technically classified as an existing staff member.

'I lost the €60,000 lump sum straight off. We had hoped to put it away for our old age – but it's just gone. The company pension has shrunk from the €390 a week I had expected to just €90. And I am not the worst. There are 1,200 other workers in the same situation. There is a glass blower I know who did not want to leave work. But if he had gone earlier, he would have received his €98,000 and a proper pension,' Tommy explained.

If Tommy Hogan had been employed in the company's sister plant in Britain, the outcome would have been different.

In 1980, the EU passed an Insolvency Directive to offer a level of protection for pension funds. A subsequent judgment in the European Court of Justice further clarified the matter and, as a result, the British government introduced a pension insurance scheme. Companies pay an annual risk-based levy to a pension protection fund and in the event of a shortfall, the state pays 90 per cent of entitlements, up to £27,770. As a result, workers from the Waterford Wedgwood sister company in Stoke on Trent will receive the bulk of their pension. But Tommy Hogan and his former workmates will get nothing beyond one-fifth of their original entitlements.

The political parties which dominate Dáil Eireann think it is too costly to give pension security to workers. Yet they apply a different standard to their own pensions because €8 million was spent on paying the pensions of ex-TDs and senators in 2008. Ray Burke, the disgraced ex-Minister, received €52,000; Charlie McCreevy, who currently receives €231,000 a year as EU Commissioner, received €52,000; Alan Dukes, who has worked as a lobbyist and PR consultant, received €54,000. The Irish parliament has never explained how it could so blatantly look after TDs while, at the same time, telling workers like Tommy Hogan to accept pension poverty. Except, maybe, by the Irish capacity to take pain.

The economic crash is hitting people in a variety of ways. Anna O'Loughlin, for example, is a 26-year-old graduate from Trinity College who now works as a primary school teacher. Like many others, she heeded advice to 'take the plunge' during the Celtic Tiger years, and bought a house for €300,000. Her three bed-roomed terraced home cost her €1,650 a month, and even with an additional rental income of €400 a month, it was a bit of a stretch on a salary of €40,000 a year. But calculations were different then in Ireland, when the property boom was in full swing.

But now the government has started hitting her with levies. As a language support teacher at St. Gabriel National School in Dublin, she is supposed to be a 'privileged' public sector worker. For months, a hate campaign has been stirred up on radio talk shows and the print media against these employees. According to John McGuinness, the then Minister of State for Trade, the public sector was 'now so protected by its unions that it has largely become a reactionary, inert mass at the centre of our economy'.[2] According to ISME, the Irish Small and Medium Enterprises Association, public sector workers have 'luxury jobs in a cushioned sector.'[3] This demonising culminated in a pension levy.

Anna O'Loughlin took a hit of €50 a week. Like all public sector workers who were employed after 1995, she already pays six and a half per cent of her salary towards her pension and so the levy was a misnomer. The revenues raised were not ring-fenced for future pensions but went into general government funds, and a small number of public employees, who do not receive a pension, were also forced to pay the levy. It was simply a wage cut, indeed a headline wage cut designed to encourage a wider reduction in living standards across the country.

This was not the only blow that Anna received. Before the pension levy was introduced, another special income levy was imposed on all PAYE workers and was made payable on gross income. It started at 1 per cent in October 2008 and then doubled in the April 2009 budget. The health levy also doubled from 2 per cent to 4 per cent, but this, too, had little to do with health as spending on hospitals was simultaneously slashed. On top of all that, the cut in spending on education closed off an opportunity for Anna to take up a promotional post, which would have been worth €4,000 a year. By the end of all these impositions, Anna O'Loughlin was in a difficult situation because she had lost over €400 a month and was paying a very high mortgage. 'I am left with €94 a week after paying my mortgage which was taken out two years ago when prices were at their peak and after paying the other bills,' Anna explained.

A young teacher and an older glass worker; one in the public sector, the other in the private sector. There are countless more who are suffering the pain that Brian Lenihan thought would have caused riots in France. The ambitions and aspirations of tens of thousands have been devastated by Ireland's worst ever economic crash. By the end of 2010, it is expected that nearly one in six workers will be unemployed. Behind those figures are real people who never visited a Social Welfare office in their lives. Architects, engineers, solicitors who once thought they had a strong middle class career ahead of them sign on alongside factory workers and builders.

There is a distinct edginess at the long queues that form at Irish post offices where people collect their meagre survival payments. 'When I go there, I feel that people are looking at me as if they are saying, what right have you got to collect money here. I hate going because you really feel what it means to be a non-national,' said Linda, a migrant from the French overseas department of Martinique. She has paid social security in Ireland for nearly ten years but it makes little difference. The categories and labels that the state uses to classify the population come spewing back when resentment grows.

No matter where they come from, social welfare recipients are suffering. But government ministers still complain that too much state money is being spent on the poor. Brian Lenihan, whose own pain has been softened by a €230,000 a year salary, has argued that social welfare recipients have never had it so good. 'When you take the 3 per cent increase [in social welfare payments] provided for this year, together with a 5 per cent drop in the cost of living that we may have, [that's] a real increase in social welfare provision of 8 per cent,' Mr Lenihan said.[4] So his attacks on social welfare payments have already begun and others are on the way. Changes to the rules on Rent Supplement have forced people to pay more to their landlords and effectively decreased their welfare payments by 5 per cent.[5] The double payment at Christmas has also been abolished, even though many desperately need it to partake in the festive season. On an annual basis, that represents another 2 per cent cut.

Those at work face increased pressure to accept wage cuts on top of the state levies. Staff in University College Cork, RTE, Sherry Fitzgerald and the Independent Groups of Newspapers are just some of the groups who have been asked to take a wage cut. The employers' organisation, Irish Business and Employers Confederation (IBEC), is actively encouraging its members to impose these wage reductions. Typically, workers are called together by their management and asked to 'voluntarily' forego a pay rise for the good of their company. Some are brought in individually, and intimidated into accepting wage cuts. Rarely is a commitment given that the cuts will be restored when profits rise. It is even rarer to get a promise that profits will be shared if the good times return.

Ireland's economic crash is having repercussions far beyond this island. One in seven Irish workers is a migrant and many have traditionally sent remittances back to their families. Remittances have become a major source of aid for developing countries and a vital lifeline that keeps absolute poverty at bay. The same occurred with Irish families in the past, when many looked forward to the American parcel. But now the thousands of Indian and Filipino nurses who are employed here face a difficulty. In the past, they were able to send up to 20 or 30 per cent of their income back to relatives, but they can barely sustain this when they face a levy of €400 a month.

The Irish crash is not unique but it is of a special proportion – in the same league as Latvia or, maybe, even Iceland. Vincent Browne recently caught the sheer scale of it, from a casual remark made by a leading economist at an ESRI press conference:

> The contraction [i.e. collapse] of the Irish economy is the worst anywhere since the Great Depression. Well, not anywhere, anywhere among the industrial countries since the Great Depression. You have to allow for countries like Zimbabwe.[6]

The reference to Zimbabwe was awesome, but the overall point was correct. There are few countries in the industrialised world which have experienced a crash of the same scale to what Ireland is undergoing today. According to the European Commission assessment, the Irish economy will shrink by 9 per cent in 2009, a magnitude that is similar to what the US experienced during the Wall Street Crash of 1929.[7] But the crash appears deeper because Ireland was, until very recently, the miracle economy of Europe, growing at the fairly spectacular annual rate of 5 per cent in 2007.[8] This level of economic growth brought rising living standards and expectations of a better life, even if it was distributed unevenly. So the speed of the change from boom to bust has left many reeling in shock.

BAIL OUTS

When people face such a huge economic trauma, they look to their government for help. But it appears that it has turned a deaf ear. No serious emergency measures have been undertaken to give people work. Even the conservative economist Jim O'Leary has expressed concern that:

> ... the official response to date essentially amounts to a proposition that restoring order to public finances, repairing our broken banking system and being lifted by the tide of global recovery, when it turns, will sort the problem.[9]

An alternative response might have been to establish a public works scheme and to expand the public sector. The logic for this intervention is utterly simple. The more people lose their jobs, the less money there is to buy goods produced by other workers. A government that actively intervened could alleviate this suffering by stepping in where private businesses are unwilling. It happened during the 1930s in the US; it occurred on a large scale in Japan in the 1990s; even today in the US President Obama talks about supporting 'shovel ready' projects to get people back to work.

But the Irish approach is different. Far from supporting employment, the state is making it worse by sacking people from the public sector. A jobs embargo has been imposed in the public sector and thousands of employees on temporary contracts are being made redundant. One area that is particularly hard hit is an already overstretched health service. Hospital beds are being cut and nurses and other staff are being let go in an effort to increase 'savings'. In the South Infirmary Victoria Hospital in Cork, for example, a 30 bed ward will be closed during summer months because, as one nurse explained, 'In order to give oncology drugs to patients, we have to close a ward'.[10]

The whole economy has entered a downward spiral because of the cuts, levies and sackings. One sign of the collapse is the manner in which government predictions have been continually overturned by ever more dire outcomes. Early in 2008, the prediction was for a spending deficit of 2.7 per cent; by September, the government was warning of a 4 per cent deficit, just over the maximum permitted under the EU Growth and Stability Pact; in the April 2009 budget, the deficit was over 10 per cent. Yet despite this downward trajectory, the government adheres to its policy of reducing living standards.

The only sector of Irish society that is being bailed out is the banks. Yet the banks have been the most rapacious element of Irish society, making huge fortunes during the Celtic Tiger years. In its 45-year history, for example, the Allied Irish Bank never made a single annual loss until the recent crisis. In the last two decades, the banks have been driven by even more fanatical desires to cut costs, hike up charges and engage in all sorts of strange behaviour to clock up the magic €1 billion in profits.

In the early 1990s, the banks colluded in the evasion of DIRT tax by accepting fictitious foreign addresses for 'non-resident' accounts. AIB's internal auditor, Tony Spollen, later estimated that his bank had aided and abetted in the theft of around £100 million from the state through its operation of bogus non-resident accounts.[11] There then followed a litany of over-charging scandals, each of which was described as an oversight. Between 1995 and 2004, for example, the AIB overcharged customers on foreign exchanges by €34 million. In 2006, the AIB announced a further €31.6 million of overcharging that had been identified subsequent to the Financial Regulator's report, making a combined total of €65.8 million.[12] According to its former group internal auditor, Eugene McErlane, his unit had reported this overcharging to the Financial Regulator in 2001 but no action on the issue emerged until a further whistleblower surfaced in 2004.[13]

Although they present themselves as staid, solid and, above all, respectable institutions, whose boards were graced with very important people, the banks engaged in the most scurrilous tactics to raise profits. In one bizarre example in 2001, AIB used its stock broking division, Goodbody Stockbrokers, to anonymously buy millions of its own shares. The transaction was routed through Nevis, a Caribbean island that is a notorious destination for tax evasion and money laundering, and one of the cheques was signed by a certain Mr. Furstenburg.[14] To the careless eye, it might appear that the brewing company was involved but the actual signatory was an individual living in Britain. The practice enabled the bank to artificially increase its share price.

After Ireland entered the euro-zone, the banks found a more systematic and dramatic way to increase profits. They borrowed vast sums from international money markets and began hyping up the property bubble. Many of the loans were lent out to a few score of property developers who had links with Fianna Fáil. Restraints on general lending were also eased, and many were actively encouraged to take out huge mortgages. The banks gained enormously from this explosion of debt, and pushed their profit margins up, as Table 1 indicates.

Table 1: Profits of Three Main Banks

	2005	2006	2007
Allied Irish Bank	€1.75 billion	€2.6 billion	€2.5 billion
Bank of Ireland	€1.393 billion	€1.7 billion	€1.794 billion
Anglo Irish Bank	€680 million	€850 million	€1.24 billion

Source: Annual Reports and Accounts

When reference is made to 'the banks' this can become an anonymous term that hides a reality of extraordinary personal greed. Only 70 directors control the six major Irish banks, and of these, 20 are executive directors and 50 are non-executive directors.[15] The executive directors play the key role in any company as they have control of day to day information. This means that 20 people made decisions that had an enormous impact on Irish society. Many were given obscene salary packages because, it was argued, they had to be 'incentivised'. An American model of hefty performance-related bonuses and payment in share options was used so that directors were encouraged to take more risks to build up the banks' profits and their own salary packages. These salaries were justified on the basis of recruiting people of the 'highest calibre' because only they had the sheer brilliance to engineer spectacular growth. However, a report from the Covered Institution Remuneration Oversight Committee, a body set up to report to the Department of Finance, noted that 'in the period of substantial growth in remuneration, there were no difficulties in recruitment – in many cases senior management appointments came from within the organisation'.[16] In other words, the salaries were driven by sheer greed.

As is evident from Table 2, many of the bank's directors also prepared a 'golden parachute' for their retirement. The most spectacular case, who is not listed as one of the big three, was Michael Fingleton, the boss of Irish Nationwide, who received a pension package of €27.6 million. When people inquired how this occurred, they were met with a 'say nothing' response. Nobody from the remuneration committee, which awarded this pension, was present at the Irish Nationwide shareholders Annual General Meeting to answer questions because they had either resigned or were sick or otherwise unavailable. When someone pointed out that the company report for 2007 had indicated that the fund was for 'members', and not just one man, it was stated that this was due to a 'typographical error'.[17]

Fingleton's pension package makes those of others look mild in comparison. Yet there is nothing moderate about the pension packages awarded to top bankers who were forced to resign. Brian Goggin, the former CEO of Bank of Ireland, for example, will retire on a €626,000 pension per year.[18] That huge sum is the equivalent of the average wage of 17 workers. The AIB boss, Eugene Sheehy, has to settle for a modest €526,000 per year, the equivalent of the average wage of 15 workers.[19] Ironically, the pensions of these 'average' workers were often invested in the banks run by Messrs Goggin and Sheehy. This occurred because there was an over-concentration by Irish-administered pension funds in the shares of Irish banks. Investment consultant Rubicon has estimated that €27 billion has been wiped off these funds, mainly as a result of this over-exposure.[20] Unless there are some big changes, many more workers will, unfortunately, suffer the same fate as Tommy Hogan and his colleagues at Waterford Crystal while the former directors live a life of some luxury.

Table 2: Total Salary Package of Annual Pension Entitlements of Executive Directors of the Big Three Banks 2007

Name of Director	Total Salary Package (€)	Annual Pension (€)	Bank
Brian Goggin	3,998,000,000	626,000	Bank of Ireland
David Drumm	3,274,000,000	258,000	Anglo Irish
Eugene Sheehy	2,105,000,000	526,000	AIB
Colm Doherty	1,663,000,000	289,000	AIB
John O Donovan	1,581,000,000	202,000	Bank of Ireland
William McAteer	1,427,000,000	94,000 (DC)	Anglo Irish
Donal Forde	1,394,000,000	275,000	AIB
Declan Quilligan	1,366,000,000	147,000	Anglo Irish
John O Donnell	1,273,000,000	261,000	AIB
Denis Donovan	1, 246,000,000	258,000	Bank of Ireland
Tom Browne	1,226,000,000	123,000 (DC)	Anglo Irish
Pat Whelan	1,212,000,000	117,000	Anglo Irish
D. Crowley	1,113,000,000	260,800	Bank of Ireland
Richie Boucher	1,015,000,000	131,700	Bank of Ireland

Source: Bank of Ireland Reports and Accounts 2007; Anglo Irish Bank Reports and Accounts 2007; Allied Irish Bank Reports and Accounts 2008. (DC indicates Defined Contribution pension scheme.)

Despite all this, the government has mobilised vast amounts of public money to shore up these banks. The state handouts came in four main steps.

First, on the night of 30 September 2008, an emergency meeting took place between Brian Cowen, Brian Lenihan and a number of prominent bankers after shares in Irish banks nose dived on the stock markets. Other cabinet members were not present but they were awoken from their sleep to hold an 'incorporeal cabinet' meeting. Stephen Collins, the usually well informed political correspondent, gave his version of what happened:

> Some of the official advice given to the Taoiseach and Lenihan favoured letting the weakest link in the banking chain fold, with the State then stepping in to acquire it as happened in Britain with Northern Rock. This line of action was supported by those advocating the 'moral hazard' argument that the taxpayer should not be asked to reward bad banking practices.
>
> However, senior politicians took the view that far from bringing an air of realism into the equation, a decision to allow one bank to go down would simply fuel further attacks on the two big banks, which are fundamentally sound.[21]

The weakest link was Anglo Irish Bank, which had experienced the biggest run on shares, but the Fianna Fáil politicians present decided that it had to be equally protected. The outcome was a government announcement that it was guaranteeing 'the deposits, loans and obligations' of all the six major Irish banks. Anglo Irish, it should be noted, had a loan book of €73.2 billion, or just under half the total size of the Irish economy for one year – so this was some guarantee.[22]

It was an attempt to gain first mover advantage by getting ahead of other countries in a cute move. The aim was to attract more funds into Irish banks during the credit crunch and so boost their shares. Gordon Brown denounced it as an aggressive measure while the German Chancellor Angela Merkel called it unacceptable. The guarantee was for €440 billion in funds, about two and a half times the size of the whole Irish economy. Later, in April 2009, when the IMF issued its Growth and Stability Report, Ireland was placed top of the list of European countries for guaranteed bank debt, ahead of far larger countries such as Germany and Britain.[23] An insurance scheme for such a large amount is costly and so the banks had to pay €445 million to the Central Bank. Yet if they had bought the same insurance policy on an open market, it would have cost an additional €425 million. In other words, the banks received a subsidy for that amount.

Second, in December 2008, the government announced that it was injecting €1.5 billion into Anglo Irish Bank. But when this did not stop its share price dropping by 98 per cent below the value for the previous year, the government nationalised it on 15 January 2009. It is sometimes assumed that nationalisation is a left wing measure, but this was nothing of the sort. If Anglo Irish had gone bankrupt, the international bond holders who had lent it money could have forced the government to honour its guarantee. They could also take control of the assets of Anglo Irish's major borrowers, the fifteen largest property developers with loans of over €500 million. The nationalisation of Anglo Irish was a way, therefore, for the state to take on Anglo's loans at a huge unforeseen cost.

Third, the government also agreed to inject a further €7 billion into Bank of Ireland and Allied Irish Bank. Public funds were used to purchase shares in banks that had huge levels of debt. The re-capitalisation of AIB consisted of €3.5 billion, which will come from the state, and €1.5 billion which will be raised by AIB itself. But the toxic debts at AIB are probably much higher than this. Analysts at J.P. Morgan, for example, have claimed that losses at Irish banks could reach €26.9 billion, and that they may require a further €12.9 billion injection of capital, in addition to the €7 billion already invested in Allied Irish Bank and Bank of Ireland.[24] In other words, even more public funds will be poured in to prop up the banks.

Fourth, on April 7, the government announced it was setting up the National Assets Management Agency to take over the management of between €80 billion and €90 billion of debt, much of it toxic. No one knows exactly how much this will cost Irish society, but as NAMA's declared purpose is to support the banks, rather than bankrupt them, that can only occur with the help of yet more public funds.

SHOCK THERAPY

Why is all this occurring? Why are the wealthy people involved in banks more important than PAYE workers like Tommy Hogan or Anna O'Loughlin?

One possible reason is that Irish banks have traditionally had a close relationship with the political elite. They mix in similar social circles and share a broadly similar outlook. Many of the political elite are also true believers in the supposedly free market and loathe the very idea of nationalisation, particularly when it has any radical connotation. Some of the non-executive directors of banks have had political connections, or once worked at the core of the state apparatus. Dermot Gleeson, for example, who was the chair of Allied Irish Bank, was a Fine Gael appointed attorney general. He was politically close to its then leader, John Bruton, and even allowed his house to be used as his headquarters during discussions on the formation of a coalition government with the Labour Party.[25] AIB's former chief executive, Michael Buckley, was once the Secretary of the Department of Social Welfare.

However, while these networks are quite tight, they hardly offer a full explanation of the government's actions in supporting banks, and doing little to stem the rise of social suffering. Other elements must also be involved in a strategy that is shared by the whole of the political establishment.

The banks are a key component of Irish capitalism. For many complex historic reasons, Irish capitalists often did not show a great desire to set up manufacturing concerns and were usually more enthusiastic about making money in property and finance. The banks, therefore, played a disproportionate role in Irish capitalism, as their dominance of the Irish Stock Exchange indicated. Many of the richest people have purchased large amounts of bank shares, and an even higher proportion of the upper middle class have invested their savings there. Banks are also deeply enmeshed in interlocking directorships that tie together blocks of Irish capital. There are clear and distinct connections between the banks and prominent Irish companies such as the Independent News and Media, Smurfit and Cement Roadstone Holdings. The banks provide huge loans to other Irish commercial concerns and, naturally, extract a high rate of profit in return. In other words, the collapse of the banks would have left a black hole within Ireland Inc.

Once the central role of banks is recognised, the options facing pro-capitalist politicians are limited. There may be some argument between the two main right wing parties about the rescue operation of Anglo Irish Bank, as its key personnel were closer to Fianna Fáil, but after the decisions taken on the night of September 30, Fine Gael had no hesitation in voting for the state guarantee scheme as much as Fianna Fáil. Internally, the parliamentary Labour Party agonised over the issue but then, after a day long debate, distanced themselves. Subsequently, they advocated the nationalisation of banks, but on the strict basis that it was only a temporary measure and did not involve the seizure of assets or the write off of toxic debt. The Labour Party also thought that banks would still be run on 'commercial lines' to guarantee private shareholders, who had a minority stake, an adequate return, even after they were nationalised. In varying ways, all the main parties assume that society must take responsibility for propping up a vital element of Irish capitalism.

That can only mean the transfer of vast resources to a small elite who are guided by the profit principle. As long as we live in a for-profit economy, nothing functions unless a big carrot of profit is available to the wealthy. In the coming years, therefore, additional funds from the population will be offered as an inducement to investors. It is like bringing gifts and performing sacrifices for gods who were thought to control our lives – except that the sacrifices are poorer health services, pension insecurity for thousands and increased levies on PAYE workers. None of this should be seen as inevitable or a mere 'acceptance of realities' – it is rather the consequence of a particular way of organising our society. If that was to change, there would be no need for this.

The other element in the government's strategy is what Naomi Klein has called the Shock Doctrine. Klein examined a number of crises that have affected different societies, from Hurricane Katrina in New Orleans to the Tiananmen Square massacre of 1989. She noted that when the populations are still reeling in shock, their rulers often take the opportunity to re-structure how they dominate society. Drastic changes take place which were inconceivable in the past, but which are deemed necessary to overcome the crisis. Usually these measures deepen inequality or lead to greater repression. The plans for these changes, however, do not simply develop out of the blue in the midst of a crisis. There is often a longer gestation where the ideas are debated in ruling class discussions before surfacing as practical proposals.

New Orleans offers a particularly poignant example. Three months after Hurricane Katrina, the then 93-year-old guru of neo-liberalism, Milton Friedman, wrote an article in the *Wall Street Journal* which noted that:

> Most New Orleans schools are in ruins as are the homes
> of the children who attended. This is a tragedy; it is also
> an opportunity to reform the education system.[26]

He saw the hurricane as an opportunity to end state-controlled schools which Friedman saw as a form of socialism. Schools should instead, he argued, be run by private corporations with public funds. Within 19 months, the unthinkable happened and Friedman's wish came true. In contrast to the slowness in dealing with the human consequence of the hurricane, the schools of New Orleans were all auctioned off to private companies.

The example has a more general application, as Klein explains:

Friedman predicted that the speed, suddenness and scope of economic shifts would provoke psychological reactions in the public that 'facilitate the adjustment'. He coined the phrase for this painful tactic: economic 'shock treatment'. In the decades since, whenever governments have imposed sweeping free-market programmes, the all-at-once shock treatment, or 'shock therapy', has been the method of choice.[27]

Ireland is presently undergoing a form of shock therapy and the script has been largely written by the employers' organisation, IBEC. Irish employers have long felt that their workers were paid too much, even though wage increases have been restrained by social partnership. Wage reductions are a rather sensitive issue and so IBEC has framed it in a language of 'competitiveness'. 'We believe that Ireland's lost competitiveness during this decade amounts to 15 per cent relative to our main trading partners,' they asserted.[28] A previous attempt to reduce wages occurred during the Irish Ferries dispute in 2005, when workers were sacked and others were hired on wages that were below the minimum wage. Although SIPTU failed to press home the advantage they won through popular mobilisation, they did enough to halt the spread of that example elsewhere.

The crash and the subsequent shock have provided IBEC with a new opportunity to impose wage cuts. The employers are quite explicit about their aims:

> We estimate that wage levels require a downward correction of the order of 10 per cent. Many companies are already taking such action; society needs to be convinced of the necessity to achieve wage reduction on an economy wide basis.... We recognise that income correction will impart a further deflationary impact on the economy in 2009 and 2010 but will be the foundation for a more bold and sustainable recovery in subsequent years.[29]

'Economy wide' wage cuts was a reference to the public sector, and IBEC was again quite explicit, demanding that 'the cost of public sector pay and expenditure on current services should be cut by 9 per cent'.[30] The purpose was to have a demonstration effect, to create a signal that the government was serious about this agenda. It would also set a clear norm that would accelerate the wage cuts that IBEC members had begun in the private sector. If wage cuts are accepted, there is a danger that workers will decide not to work for lower rates and it is equally necessary to cut social welfare to force them to do so. Once again, IBEC offered a very specific target:

> Irish social welfare must be fundamentally reappraised in the light of the predicted decline in living standards. All social welfare rates should therefore be reduced by 3 per cent in the April [2009] Supplementary Budget. [31]

IBEC's main concern is to garner full political support for this strategy. It faced some difficulties because Fianna Fáil has a populist base, and its TDs often present themselves as defenders of social welfare recipients at local level. The crash was an opportunity, however, to change this outlook and put some bourgeois backbone into these populists. Claiming to draw on an international experience, IBEC argued that:

> The most politically sensitive components of government spending, transfer payments [i.e. social welfare] and government wages have been cut during successful adjustments.... Since the cuts that will be the most effective are also the most politically sensitive, communication is paramount.

This agenda has been reproduced almost word for word by Fianna Fáil ministers. IBEC's demand for a 10 per cent cut across the board was echoed by Brian Cowen when he spoke to a business audience at the Dublin Chamber of Commerce. He claimed that living standards would have to fall by between 10 and 12 per cent but that we must still 'stick together as a community'.[32] IBEC's call for a cut in public sector pay had already been answered by the pension levy, which was merely a device to get around the legal difficulties associated with changing contracts of employment. Its demand for a 3 per cent cut in social welfare was answered by the withdrawal of the Christmas bonus and a decrease in Rent Supplement.

All of this goes some way to explaining why the government is rescuing banks while letting unemployment figures escalate. It can no longer hide behind a mantra of not interfering in a market economy, but its interference is mainly designed to help the wealthy. It knows that its levies and pay cuts have a deflationary effect which will lead to more unemployment because even IBEC acknowledged that 'income correction' would cause that. However, if the strategy is to reduce Irish wages, then rising unemployment has a certain advantage. As Margaret Thatcher found when she allowed unemployment to more than double in her first years of office, it provides a fertile ground to re-engineer society and create more compliant workers.

The social suffering is, therefore, not accidental. It is not merely the product of a corrupt, ignorant or even 'uncaring' government. It will be carried out by Fine Gael as well as Fianna Fáil. It is nothing less than the price being paid to preserve Irish capitalism.

GLOBAL CAPITALISM

It is also a price being exacted from people all over the world. Global capitalism has entered the deepest recession that it has ever experienced since WWII. It was triggered by a collapse in the US financial system where deeper structural problems were also involved. Early hopes that some of the major developing countries such as China and India could de-couple from the US economy and provide an engine to pull the world out of a downturn proved false. Instead, the downturn has spread right across the world, like a contagion pulling down economy after economy.

Most conventional economists are at a loss to explain why it has happened. Of the 15,000 professional economists who work in the US, only about twelve are reported to have foreseen the recession coming.[33] The reason is that modern economics has largely become a discipline that is supportive of free markets. As the markets supposedly bring supply and demand into equilibrium, economic crises of the scale Ireland and the world are currently experiencing were barely conceivable.

Since the crisis broke, two new responses have emerged as possible explanations. One suggests that it was caused by excessive risk taking and reckless behaviour by the financial markets. In other words, that the balance had swung too far towards deregulation, and that greater state intervention can bring a return to normality. But this does little to explain why financial services came to play such a dominant role in the US and other economies. It also takes little account of how corporations were able to become so powerful that they could spend millions lobbying politicians to get their own way. There are also no grounds for thinking that steady, consistent growth rates of the scale that occurred in the past will return.

Another explanation looks to human psychology and its impact on economies. According to Akerlof and Schiller, conventional economists assumed that people functioned rationally and so they missed out on a vital aspect of their behaviour – their animal spirits.[34] Such spirits include trust and confidence in others, a sense of fairness and, on the more negative side, a propensity to corruption and anti-social behaviour. These spirits were excessively high before the crash as people trusted in banks and developed quite a selfish outlook. As long as those spirits kept up, they drove the global economy forward. Now, however, the same animal spirits have flagged and swung in the opposite direction. Trust has disappeared and there is a reluctance to invest money in ways that allows the system to function effectively.

One consequence of Akerlof and Schiller's analysis is a belief that a recovery can be talked up because it will get those animal spirits moving again. The Obama regime, in particular, has made huge efforts to accentuate the positive. Every minor sign of an up-turn – from retail sale figures in New York to bank stress tests – are used to herald the return of the green shoots recovery.

The problem with the wider analysis, however, lies in separating cause and effect. The confidence of bankers and industrialists in their ability to make money broke down during the crash. But it might be equally argued that this arises from a breakdown of the system itself. The pursuit of profit is the main driver for why investment is made and, as a consequence, why people are employed. As long as profit levels are high, the system appears to work, even if its rewards are distributed unequally. But when profitability falls and problems arise in the balance between production and consumption, capitalism faces a crisis. 'The animal spirits' merely reflect these shifts rather than being their primary cause.

Capitalism can, of course, recover from the crash but it does so through a form of economic cannibalism. When enough bankruptcies have occurred, the surviving firms can buy them up cheaply and gain extra profits. At that point, they will hope to have driven down wages and the prices of raw materials. But even after all the suffering, another crash will occur at some future point. This current crash, after all, is only the latest of a long line of other less severe crashes.

The choice facing us, therefore, is whether we sacrifice our living standards and our futures in the vague hope that the system will re-generate itself on a sustained basis – or do we look for real alternatives? This book proposes the latter approach and to do so, it shifts between the global and local dimensions of the crash. It looks at solutions to the Irish economic crash but also recognises that they will only be effective if there is a wider challenge to the system itself. Its aim is to lay the basis for a radical agenda of change.

Endnotes

[1] 'Europe 'amazed' at steps taken in Budget – Lenihan' *Irish Times*, 27 April 2009.

[2] 'Union calls on Minister to retract "outrageous remark", *Irish Times,* 16 September 2008.

[3] 'ISME calls for 30,000 public sector job cuts', ISME Press Release, 16 October 2008.

[4] ' Government flags further welfare cuts', *Irish Tines,* 23 April 2009.

[5] INOU Press Statement, 'Unemployment must become the government's top priority', 29 April 2009.

[6] 'Ireland's uniquely steep slump is down to us', *Irish Times,* 29 April 2009.

[7] European Commission, *Economic Forecast Spring 2009* (Brussels: EU Commission, 2009) p. 63.

[8] ibid. p. 63.

[9] 'Unemployment threatens to become a catastrophe', *Irish Times,* 15 May 2009.

[10] 'Hospital to close ward to pay for drugs, nurses told', *Irish Times,* 8 May 2009.

[11] 'Laughing all the way at the bank', *Sunday* Tribune, 25 March 2001.

[12] 'Raw Deal from Banks', *Sunday Business Post,* 8 January 2006.

[13] 'Did the regulator fail to act on AIB', *Sunday Business Post,* 5 April 2009.

[14] 'AIB to explain handling of irregular share deals', *Irish Examiner,* 8 April 2009.

[15] Financial Regulator, *Disclosure of Directors Loans in Covered Institutions* (Dublin: Financial Regulator 2009) p. 8.

[16] Covered Institution Remuneration Oversight Committee, *Report to Minister for Finance,* 27 February 2009, p. 10.

[17] 'All fingers point to the absent Fingleton in cries for answers', *Irish Independent,* 13 May 2008.

[18] 'Why Fingleton pension pig-out adds insult to our injury', *Evening Herald,* 25 March 2009.

[19] Ibid.

[20] Rubicon Press Release, 6 January 2009.

[21] 'State intervention yields at least short term gain', *Irish Times,* 1 October.

[22] 'Worries Over Anglo Irish exposure in the US', *Sunday Business Post*, 11 January 2009.

[23] IMF, *Growth and Stability Report*, April 2009, p. 49.

[24] 'EBS takes pain up front with loan write off', *Irish Times*, 13 March 2009.

[25] 'Sharpest knife in the drawer', *Sunday Business Post*, 2 September 2001.

[26] N. Klein, *The Shock Doctrine: The Rise of Disaster Capitalism* (London: Allen Lane, 2007), pp. 4-5.

[27] Ibid, p. 7.

[28] IBEC, *Supplementary Budget Proposals* (Dublin: IBEC, 2009) p. 4.

[29] Ibid, p. 4.

[30] Ibid, p. 12.

[31] Ibid, p. 13.

[32] 'Cowen warning on living standards', *Irish Times*, 7 February 2009.

[33] The figure is James Galbraith's. See 'The Populist', *New York Times*, 31 October 2008.

[34] G.A. Akerlof and R. Schiller, *Animal Spirits: How Psychology Drives the Economy and Why it Matters for Global Capitalism* (Princeton: Princeton University Press, 2009).

1

REMEMBER THE CELTIC TIGER?

U NTIL RECENTLY IRELAND WAS KNOWN as the Celtic Tiger, a miracle economy that was admired and marvelled at all around the world. Economies are deemed to be successful if they grow by an extra 2 or 3 per cent a year, and Ireland was described as a Tiger economy because its growth rates were often three times that level. Apart from one brief interlude, the Celtic Tiger economy sustained high growth rates from its inception in 1995 to its demise in 2008.

The Irish success story was hailed as proof that the 'Washington Consensus' worked. This consensus involved a series of measures devised by economists who argued against 'interference in the free market'. Specifically, they claimed that if taxes on capital were cut, if there was full freedom to repatriate profits, if state enterprises were privatised and social spending cut back, if there was 'light touch' regulation – then a country would become an economic success story. They pointed to a poor country on the edge of Europe which had followed these textbook recipes to become the envy of the world. The fervour in some quarters for the Celtic Tiger knew no bounds.

Thomas Friedman, a columnist with the *New York Times*, praised Ireland as the 'leapin leprechaun' and recommended that 'old Europe' change its ways to catch up with it.[1] In a similar vein, a US think tank, the Cato Institute, published a major article to prove that the Celtic Tiger succeeded because it embraced 'eco-

nomic freedom'.[2] The Heritage Foundation, a think tank funded
by Exxon Mobil, Chevron Texaco and Merrill Lynch, awarded Ireland fifth place in its global 'freedom' index, significantly higher
than the US itself.[3] Nicholas Vardy, who is described as a 'global
guru' for investors, claimed that:

> Ireland is already richer than France or Germany, yet its
> growth rates remain triple that of its larger rivals. Fa-
> vourable tax policies, a welcoming environment for For-
> eign Direct Investment, and a highly educated 21st cen-
> tury work force will ensure that the Celtic Tiger will con-
> tinue to roar for many years to come.[4]

Irish politicians lapped up this praise and repeated the mantras. The Irish people, they claimed, had to stick together to de-
fend their right to provide a tax haven for global corporations. If
scams could be devised to help corporations pretend more profits
were made in Ireland for tax purposes, all the better. The cry was
that 'they provided us with jobs' and so it was our patriotic duty
to help them.

This political discourse drew on a longer-term shift in Irish republican ideology. Instead of rhetoric about re-taking the 'fourth
green' field, Fianna Fáil transformed 26 county republicanism into
the small change of economic nationalism. The colonisation of Ireland, it was implied, gave its people the right to take whatever
measures were necessary to resume their rightful place in the
global economy. And since what was 'good for business was good
for Ireland', it could break all the rules to help its corporate
friends.

The union leaders were drawn into this consensus through a
system of social partnership that was devised by Charles
Haughey. For two decades, the unions urged their members not
to press for high wage rises but to settle instead for 'moderate'
increases, knowing that these could be subsidised by income tax
cuts from the state. The union leaders joined agencies such as the

National Competitiveness Council to discuss ways in which the productivity of their members could be raised, with little extra cost to employers.

Yet there was a dark side to the success story of the Celtic Tiger. During the boom years Ireland became one of the most unequal societies in the world, modelled on its mentor, the United States. Market freedom meant that those with capital or property could hike up prices and profits, while wages were restrained by social partnership. Even though incomes rose during the boom, the share of the economy allocated to wages declined faster than the EU average, as Table 1.1 indicates.

Table 1.1: Adjusted Wage Share of the Total Economy (compensation per employee as percentage of GDP at factor cost per person employed)

	EU-15	Ireland
1960-1970	n/a	77.9
1971- 1980	74.5	75.9
1980-1990	71.8	71.2
1991-2000	68.7	62.3
2001-2007	67.3	54.0

Source: European Commission Statistical Annex of European Economy, 2008, Table 32.

The combination of income tax cuts and reduced taxes on profits meant that the total tax take in Ireland was only 30 per cent of GDP, compared to an EU average of 40 per cent.[5] This meant that there was less money available for education, public transport, health and local authorities than in other countries. Nowhere was this more evident than in the health system. Maev Ann Wren has chronicled the effects of this historic under spending, even at the height of the Celtic Tiger.

Irish waiting lists compare poorly with those in other states. The UK's NHS, despite its well-publicised difficulties, does remarkably better. In September 2002 in England, only six patients in total had waited longer than 18 months for either in-patient or day treatment. Only three patients in every 10,000 had waited over a year. This compared to 21 adult patients in every 10,000 people who had waited for over a year in the Republic. In France, there are, quite simply, no waiting lists. All surgery is planned under a booking system, in which a patient is given a date for surgery immediately it is prescribed, although this may involve a few months' wait.[6]

Unfortunately, scandalous under-funding was not confined to health. Despite changes in Irish family life, the state refused to support a proper childcare system. Even though the National Economic and Social Forum recommended the establishment of a universal pre-school education, the state preferred the more inefficient method of subsiding private crèches. As a result, an official report, *Forum on the Workplace of the Future*, noted that Ireland's childcare costs were the highest in Europe and consumed a larger proportion of parents' income than elsewhere.[7] Despite rhetoric about creating a knowledge society, Ireland also had the second highest primary school class sizes in Europe. In secondary schools, 91 per cent of schools did not have a laboratory technician, restricting the ability of children to do scientific experiments and forcing them into a mode of rote learning.[8]

These were some of the most visible failures of the Celtic Tiger years, but a time bomb had also been laid by reduced spending on social protection. Table 1.2 illustrates the divergence between Europe and Ireland.

While there was full employment, funding for social protection did not seem to matter. But for pension provision, there were dramatic long-term consequences.

Table 1.2: Total Expenditure on Social Protection in % of GDP at Current Prices

	1991	1994	1997	2000	2002
EU-15	26.1	28.0	27.8	27.2	27.9
Ireland	19.6	19.7	16.6	14.3	16.0

Source: Europe in Figures, Eurostat Year book 2005.

During the boom, Ireland maintained one of the lowest levels of spending on pensions, at only 3.7 per cent of GDP as against, at the other extreme, 14.7 per cent in Italy.[9] The general buoyancy in revenues allowed the state to pay an old age state pension of over €200 a week, but no pressure was exerted on employers to contribute to proper schemes for their workers. In the private sector, coverage dropped to an abysmal 38 per cent of employees, and there was a shift from defined benefit schemes to defined contribution schemes.[10] In the former case, employers are obliged to fund a definite proportion of an ex-employee's income on retirement, but in the latter, a pension fund is invested in the stock exchanges and the employee carries the risk if these go wrong. This, unfortunately, is precisely what happened.

As long as the boom lasted, most workers were not overly concerned about these problems. Many despised the political elite as revelations about corruption reached a crescendo. But the past experiences of emigration and unemployment gave the boom a sweet taste, and, while the deficiencies were recognised, they were also effectively ignored.

FIANNA FÁIL

This helps explain both the extraordinary success of Fianna Fáil and the problems it now faces with the collapse of the Celtic Tiger. The party is one of the great peculiarities of European politics because it has a working class voting base even though it pursues policies that blatantly benefit the wealthy. This historic anachronism resulted from the way it originally challenged Ireland's neo-colonial status after it left the British empire. In the 1920s, when the forerunners of Fine Gael were content to govern Ireland as 'an out-garden of Britain',[11] Fianna Fáil constructed an industrial bloc that linked native business leaders with the workers movement. They demanded full political and economic independence and were de-fined by militant republican opposition to imperialism. For a pe-riod, they used left wing rhetoric to win support from trade union-ists, and even promised to abolish the banks and replace them with a credit union system.[12] But once they took office, from 1932 on-wards, they forged a conservative alliance with the bishops, and used the rhetoric of social Catholicism to talk only of looking after the 'deserving' poor. The absence of a real left alternative allowed the party to pose as a champion of the 'plain people' of Ireland.

Cracks in this façade developed when revelations about Charlie Haughey's dealings with the business class emerged. The self-styled leader of the 'plain people' lived the lifestyle of a millionaire, with the help of the Ansbacher slush fund, established by the richest people in Ireland. The Allied Irish Bank wrote off his debts; Ben Dunne gave him £2 million in donations; and the Taoiseach, who was telling his people to 'tighten their belts', was receiving an addi-tional £5,500 a week in 'personal donations' between 1988 and 1991.[13] Just as revelations about child abuse shook the Catholic Church to its foundations, the same appeared to threaten Fianna Fáil. The party was only saved through a combination of political astuteness and good luck.

The astuteness came with social partnership. Social partner-ship allowed Fianna Fáil to preserve its caring image, even while it looked after the interests of the richest sections of society. But it also brought more tangible benefits when the party ran into diffi-culties, as the contrast between how Ireland and Italy dealt with their corruption scandals shows.[14] In 1992, Italy was struck by the *tangentopoli* scandal, where revelations about bribes to politicians emerged. This was of a similar order of magnitude to the revelations in Ireland, but in Italy there were huge union protests. Over 50,000 demonstrated in Milan and 300,000 protested in Rome, where they burnt effigies of government leaders, who they denounced as robbers. These mobilisations helped lead to the demise of the Christian Democrats, a party that resembled Fianna Fáil in its dominance of government office, and in its leadership style. (The Italian Christian Democrats were led, at one stage, by Andreotti who had, it seems, links to the Sicilian mafia).[15] But in Ireland, the unions refused to call any mobilisations against corruption because they were so tied into social partnership.

The other factor that saved Fianna Fáil was the Celtic Tiger. After the return of mass emigration in the 1980s, the boom was warmly welcomed by workers because it allowed them to buy new cars, go on foreign holidays and eat out in restaurants in ways never dreamt of before. As long as it lasted, they were willing to forgive Bertie Ahern's blatant support for his wealthy friends and his association with Haughey. Yet, even though Fianna Fáil dominated the boom years, a more subtle transformation was also underway. The party had, in fact, entered a long period of decline even though many barely recognised the signs. Three major weaknesses underlay the apparent success story of Fianna Fáil during the Celtic Tiger years.

First, the long-term decline in Fianna Fáil's share of votes continued. During the period of Jack Lynch's leadership (1966–1979) and Charles Haughey's leadership (1979–1992), the party won 48 per cent and 45 per cent of the national electorate respectively. But during the leadership of Bertie Ahern (1994–2008), which coincided almost exactly with the Celtic Tiger, the party's support declined further to 41 per cent.

Secondly, the party increasingly depended on vote transfers and an extra bonus of seats compared to its votes to return to office. The party's association with economic success allowed it to dispel the attitude of 'anybody but Fianna Fáil' among its opponents. The party also received a disproportionate share of seats compared to the percentage of votes it attracted. After the 2007 election, for example, it gained 47 per cent of Dáil seats in return for 41 per cent of votes.

Third, during the boom years a more 'instrumentalist' orientation developed among Irish voters. According to a study of the 2002 election results by Michael Marsh, Ireland came at the very bottom of a league table of 13 Western European countries for identification with particular parties. In 1981, less than 40 per cent of the electorate reported that they had no fixed party attachment, but by 2002 this had risen to three-quarters.[16] This shift is particularly damaging to Fianna Fáil, as strong party loyalty was often transmitted by families.

The sudden collapse of the Celtic Tiger has, therefore, huge consequences for Irish society at many different levels. It is shaking the very foundations of the Fianna Fáil party which has dominated Irish politics since 1932.

HOW THE TIGER GREW

The seeds of destruction of the Celtic Tiger were planted in its original success story. Contrary to the mythologies spun by economists, the Celtic Tiger did not result from a deliberate policy of privatisation, deregulation and tax cuts. If this 'hard medicine' brought its own rewards, then African countries would be booming because they were subjected to Structural Adjustment Programmes which forced them to adopt more extreme versions of the measures applied in Ireland. The same occurred in much of Latin America and Eastern Europe after the collapse of the Berlin Wall. So the obvious question is – why did only a small number of countries like Ireland become success stories?

Ireland benefited from a unique combination of circumstances, which are only now unravelling. Some of these factors had to do with developments at the level of global capitalism and others with local conditions.

In 1992, the EU established itself as a single market that allowed for the free movement of goods, services and capital inside its borders. The formation of an EU single market was part of a wider pattern of creating free trade areas around dominant economic powers – similar to the North American Free Trade Area (NAFTA). The European single market was designed to give extra advantages to European firms by allowing them to enjoy economies of scale, unified standards and a larger consumer market. However, once the single market was created, non-European corporations began to establish production facilities inside the EU in order to gain access. As a result, from the early 1990s onwards, there was a pool of foreign investment seeking a location inside the EU. US companies raced to get into the market and gain advantage over their Japanese rivals in areas like office equipment and computers. Whereas in 1985 the EU share of global foreign direct investment had fallen to 31 per cent, it rose again to 42 per cent by 1990 and remained at 39 per cent in 1995.[17] Ireland's success lay in attracting a vastly disproportionate share of US investment that was bound for Europe and so the most interesting question is – Why?

Quite clearly, there were a host of factors at work such as pay levels, educational attainments, a stable right-wing political structure and an English-speaking culture. However, one issue stands out over all others: Ireland's tax regime. From 1980s onwards, Ireland applied a 10 per cent rate of corporation tax to all enterprises in manufacturing. Later, in 1987, it extended this to financial companies operating out of the Irish Financial Services Centre. Then in 1996, it announced that it would move to a 12.5 per cent tax rate for all firms from 2003 in order to comply with EU rules.

The 12.5 per cent rate of corporation tax on profits was only the headline figure designed to attract global corporations. Ireland also provided a host of other measures to further reduce tax on profits such as, for example, tax exemptions for intellectual property or allowing corporations to write off past losses against future profits. In reality, the country re-branded itself as an Atlantic tax haven for global corporations who wanted to escape tax rates of 35 per cent on profits in the US or most of the EU. Most crucially, it had no legislation to outlaw transfer pricing. This is a practice where multinational companies manipulate the internal prices of their components in order to declare higher profits in countries which act as tax havens.

Ireland's status as both an Atlantic tax haven and a suitable location for manufacturing inside the EU made it a magnet for US factories, which sprouted up all around the country. But there was also an inflation in the profit figures from these companies due to transfer pricing. Between 1999 and 2002, for example, profits from US companies in Ireland doubled from $13.4 billion to $26.8 billion. One of the reasons for this was that a new double taxation agreement was signed with the US in 1997, which widened opportunities for avoiding US taxes. The Irish government succeeded in effectively exempting items such as royalties, profits earned from international transport and interest from tax. Similarly, it was agreed to reduce the normal US withholding tax on dividends from 30 per cent to 15 per cent in some cases, and 5 per cent in others.[18]

US tax expert Martin O'Sullivan has argued that a 'seismic shift' occurred in the late 1990s in international taxation as subsidiaries of US corporations declared 58 per cent of their profits earned abroad to be in tax havens like Ireland or Bermuda. Ireland differs from Bermuda in that real business activity takes place here – as against being purely a location for front companies. This allowed Ireland to style itself as a more respectable destination for corporations to slip below the radar screen of public opprobrium. As a result, according to O'Sullivan, Ireland came to top the list of global tax havens for US companies.[19]

The secret behind the success of the Celtic Tiger can thus be summarised succinctly: Ireland was able to get away with tax dumping inside the EU because of its tiny size and its previous underdeveloped status. It benefited from Europe's social model as regional aid flowed in to assist it to overcome underdevelopment, but it then undercut that model by introducing the lowest rate of corporation tax in the EU. Few EU governments originally objected because it took such a small share of foreign direct investment. Later, of course, there were calls for tax harmonisation and a greater scrutiny of its status as a tax haven.

TWO PHASES OF THE CELTIC TIGER

The Celtic Tiger, which grew out of this unique combination of factors, can really be divided into two phases. These phases are marked by quite different rates of growth and, more fundamentally, a dramatic shift in the nature of capital investment and economic activity.

Phase 1: 1995–2002

In the first phase, the boom was fuelled by a surge of US investment in manufacturing, producing computers, pharmaceuticals and medical devices. In 1998, the IDA could claim that 26 per cent of all the greenfield sites of US companies in Europe were located in Ireland.[20] At this stage, the amount of US capital deployed per worker was seven times the EU average.[21] As a result, Ireland quickly moved to the top of the global league for countries that are most dependent on US investment. One illustration of that dependency today is that a staggering 90 per cent of Irish exports come from foreign owned firms, principally US firms. At one stage, it was said that Viagra accounted for nearly 10 per cent of those figures.

The influx of capital investment led to a major rise in productivity. In 1970, productivity in Ireland, as measured by GNP per head, was only 62 per cent of EU levels and 42 per cent of US levels. By the year 2000, productivity was equivalent to the EU level and had reached 70 per cent of the US levels.[22] These higher levels of productivity had important social consequences. Broadly speaking, companies with high productivity can afford to pay higher wages because they gain more profits. US firms, therefore, came to be seen as 'good employers' who paid better wages than indigenous firms and this, in turn, allowed them to keep union organisation out of their plants.

This was a major change in their strategy towards Irish workers. After a huge battle in the late 1960s at the EI plant in Shannon, a subsidiary of General Electric, the IDA pressurised US companies into sweetheart deals with the Irish Transport and General Workers Union, the forerunners of SIPTU. Companies had to recognise unions but workers could only join the ITGWU which had committed itself in advance not to interfere with 'management prerogatives'. This policy changed in the 1980s when most of the major US companies such as Intel, Hewlett Packard and IBM actively discouraged unions. They succeeded because they paid relatively higher wages and because the union leaders did not want to rock the boat of national economic development.

One consequence was a dramatic decline in union membership in the private sector. By 2005, it was estimated that union density in the overall private sector was 20 per cent and only 11 per cent in the foreign-owned multinational sector. It remained, however, at over 85 per cent in the public sector.[23] This divergence between public and private sectors created the potential for division between workers, which the employers were quick to exploit after the crash.

The dominance of US investment also laid the basis for a neo-liberal ideology that was widely diffused throughout the population by the political establishment. Few dared to challenge Ireland's status as a tax haven, as it appeared to bring real benefits to the population at large. But this sentiment was used to warn against any progressive advance. Demands for environmental controls or proper labour standards were met with the claim that 'it would scare away the multinationals'. Even when the anti-war movement challenged the use of Shannon airport by US troops, it was claimed that any restriction would lead to a loss of US investment.

Yet the success story could not last. In 2001, the US economy entered a recession after a ten-year period of growth and Ireland was heavily exposed. The recession was a signal that deeper structural problems would arise from Ireland's over-dependence on US investment. Although it is difficult to draw straight lines that differentiate one period from another, we can broadly state that the first phase of the Celtic Tiger came to an end with the 2001 recession as two major problems developed which would later come back to haunt Irish society.

First, employment in manufacturing declined as US investment slowed down or moved elsewhere. Table 1.3 shows the drop in manufacturing employment after the recession of 2001.

Table 1.3: Employment in Manufacturing Industry

Year	Number
1995	217,000
1996	221,800
1997	234,600
1998	241,300
1999	239,600
2000	248,600
2001	251,000
2002	239,300
2003	230,000
2004	223,200
2005	220,000
2006	224,000
2007	223,400

Source: P. Sweeney, *Ireland's Economic Success* (Dublin: New Island, 2008), pp. 198-199.

Even before the present crash, manufacturing employment had returned to nearly the same level it was at the start of the boom – even though the labour force had expanded considerably. Today manufacturing represents just 13 per cent of the Irish workforce and the country has largely become a services economy. The ending of phase one of the Celtic Tiger meant that the promise of a high productivity, high wage economy also came to a close. In his study on Irish productivity, Paul Tansey shows that the productivity per worker typically grew by over 4 per cent a year up to 2000 but then declined to around 2.5 per cent a year after that. Productivity in manufacturing continued to rise but productivity in services actually declined by 7 per cent in the decade between 1995 and 2005.[24]

Some commentators presented the decline of manufacturing as a normal feature of an economy that matures by shifting from making goods to providing services. But there was much more involved because Ireland's unique status as a tax haven inside EU borders was being undermined. Today, for example:

- Hungary has a tax rate of 10 per cent of the first 5 million Hungarian Forint of income and 16 per cent after that.

- Estonia allows permanent establishments of non-resident companies, which are registered with the authorities, not to pay tax on their income

- Latvia has a tax rate of 15 per cent on profits, with even lower rates inside special economic zones

- Lithuania has a 15 per cent standard corporation tax but a 100 per cent exemption from all tax for six years inside economic zones and a 50 per cent for an additional 10 years, if certain conditions are met.[25]

Dell became a symbol of the decline of Irish manufacturing. The company was one of the largest US employers in Ireland, contributing, according to some estimates, 5 per cent to its GNP.[26] But while it took full advantages of Ireland's generous subsidies, it played the globalisation game by pitting workers and states against each other. In 2008, it moved its main production facility from Limerick to Lodz when it saw a chance to gain higher profits. The average industrial wage in Lodz is €7,500 a year in contrast to the Irish average of €37,500 – or, to put it differently, one-fifth of Irish wages. Since 2004, the Polish rate of corporation tax has been cut to 19 per cent, and in the special economic zones like those in Lodz there are further exemptions available from property taxes and generous grants.

Dell illustrated the flaw in Ireland's economic model. It undercut its rivals by offering a tax haven to global corporations to boost their profits, and encouraged them to cheat other governments out of tax revenue. It did everything to facilitate their needs through a 'frictionless' relationship with the IDA. But this has only triggered off a quickening of the race to the bottom and the corporations used the Irish concessions to pressurise other states to offer even more. While Ireland won the first lap of the race, it began to flag in other rounds.

The second major problem arose from Ireland's location as a centre for transfer pricing. US corporations, who artificially declared higher rates of profit in Ireland, began to withdraw ever more money in repatriations. The sheer scale meant that Irish economic figures became unreliable and this helps to explain the gap which exists between Gross Domestic Product – which includes income that is eventually lost through repatriation – and Gross National Product, which excludes it. In 2007, the former figure was 18 per cent higher than the latter and this was often used to claim that Ireland had overtaken countries like Germany or France. However, this overstated by about one-sixth how much economic activity is actually created in Ireland. Table 1.4 illustrates the huge growth in profit repatriation in more recent years.

Table 1 4: Profit Repatriation, 1995–2007

Year	Net Factor Income to the Rest of World (€ millions)
1995	–5,948
1996	–6,535
1997	–8,040
1998	–9,382
1999	–12,944
2000	–14,750
2001	–18,295
2002	–23,696
2003	–21,724
2004	–22,879
2005	–24,903
2006	–24,830
2007	–29,393

Source: CSO National Income and Expenditure Series.

By the end of the first phase of the Celtic Tiger, the surge of US investment in manufacturing came to a close and Ireland began to shift to a services economy. Its status as a tax haven and as a base for transfer pricing meant that greater amounts of capital – real or fictional – left the country. At the end of 2001, as they surveyed the problems that had arisen, the Irish government could have adopted a different approach to development. Instead, they further retrenched into the neoliberal model, and took a gamble that has fallen apart today.

Phase 2: 2002–2008

The second phase of the Celtic Tiger began after the 2001-2 recession, and was characterised by lower rates of growth. Between 1995 and 2002, GDP rose by 8.6 per cent whereas from 2002 until the crash of 2008, it rose by 5.5 per cent. The latter was still an impressive figure but the problem was the source of the growth. During phase two of the Celtic Tiger, Ireland was principally reconfigured as an enormous building site and a centre of 'financial engineering'. Both fed into each other to produce a distorted economy driven by tax breaks, political connections and debt.

A growing academic literature has recently emerged in the US on 'financialisation'.[27] This is defined as a process whereby a greater proportion of economic activity and profit comes from financial activities rather than production. Sometimes this is presented as a distinct 'regime of accumulation' that can be distinguished from a Fordist regime that relies on the mass production of consumer goods.[28] This approach, however, tends to overstate the separation between corporations engaged in finance and production. It also often fails to grasp how financialisation is rooted in deeper problems in contemporary global capitalism, as Chapter 3 will outline. For the moment, however, we will simply illustrate how Ireland represented a classic case of financialisation.

The transformation was dramatic as Ireland moved from a society where a new industrial revolution appeared to be occurring to one where more people were employed in finances rather than in factories. By 2008, 14 per cent of the Irish labour force worked in finance, as against 13 per cent in manufacturing. Financial services accounted for 10 per cent of Ireland's GDP and for one-third of its service exports. A huge proportion of native capital was channelled through finance and property.

Financialisation was driven, first, by the growth of banking in the Irish economy. On the small Irish Stock Exchange, the three main banks – alongside CRH and Ryanair – accounted for nearly

60 per cent of its capitalisation. Bank assets grew so fast that, by 2008, they exceeded Ireland's GDP by a factor of nine.[29] The banks were able to expand so quickly because the state allowed them to maintain one of the lowest bank capitalisation ratios in Western Europe. By December 2008, the ratio of bank capital and reserves to total assets was only 4.3 per cent.[30]

The expansion of the banks grew directly out of a culture of light touch regulation by the Central Bank and the Financial Regulator. Even while the banks raced ahead on the equivalent of a low fuel reserve, the governor of the Central Bank, John Hurley, was cheerfully proclaiming that 'the Irish financial system's shock absorption capacity remains robust and the system is well placed to cope with emerging issues'.[31]

The Financial Regulator, Patrick Neary, defined his philosophy of regulation as a 'principles approach' which assumed there was 'mutual trust between ourselves and the industry'. Businesses were assured that there was little to fear from an Irish regulator: 'We want to have proportionate regulation, to allow time for the industry to manage and embed change and we want to enforce compliance in a reasonable way,' Neary explained.[32]

This culture was not solely created by a few individuals such as John Hurley and Patrick Neary but went to the very heart of the Irish state. In 2004, for example, the government issued a White Paper on Better Regulation, where it baldly stated that 'we will regulate as lightly as possible given the circumstances and use more alternatives'.[33] These alternatives include 'co-regulation', which meant 'sharing the regulatory role between the regulated authority and the regulated groups', and 'performance-based regulation', where 'firms and individual are allowed to choose the process by which they comply with the law'.[34] The Irish state positively celebrated deregulation and saw itself as a major beneficiary of the new 'freedoms' it gave the Irish economy.

Nowhere was this more evident than in the way that it marketed the Irish Financial Services Centre (IFSC) to foreign investors. The message was utterly clear: if you wanted somewhere that had the aura of respectability but where there was 'full market freedom', then come to Ireland. When marketing the IFSC, the Industrial Development Authority explicitly boasted that 'there is no transfer pricing legislation' and 'no thin capitalisation rules'.[35] It stated that 'Ireland uses an Anglo-Saxon business model' and has 'proactive Private–Public Industry Forums'.[36] These forums ensured that the needs of the financial industry were catered for through direct contact with state officials.

Any proposed policy change related to the IFSC was first channelled to the Department of the Taoiseach and a special IFSC Clearing House Group. This was a group dominated by representatives of the largest banks and hedge funds, including AIB Capital Markets, Merrill Lynch, State Street International and the legal firms that serviced them. No representatives from trade unions or NGOs were allowed to participate in this group for fear they might raise any demands for re-distribution of wealth. Financial Services Ireland, a lobby group linked to the employers' organisation Irish Business and Employers Confederation, was so pleased that they acknowledged that Ireland had 'an efficient and responsive pro-business regulatory environment'. They boasted that the Financial Regulator 'consults with and reports progress to stakeholders' and 'refines the regulatory system to ensure it is a competitive and effective supervisors regime'.[37]

The IFSC played an important role in the orgy of speculation that overtook the world in the last decade. It became a major centre for the securitisation, re-insurance and hedge fund markets.

Securitisation is a term used in 'financial engineering' to reduce risk. Packages of mortgages, for example, are created by mixing those purchased by more risky households with those from less risky ones, and it was assumed that the mixture itself guaranteed security. In fact, the reverse occurred. The securitisation of sub-prime lending helped to spread the 'contagion' of the US property market throughout the global economy. The absence of regulation in centres like the IFSC allowed corporations to create ever more complex 'instruments' that hid the real nature of risk.

Secondly, the IFSC became a favoured location for the re-insurance industry. This developed after Hurricane Andrew devastated southern Florida and Louisiana in 1992 and cost the insurance companies dearly. Re-insurance involves selling 'sophisticated' products to other insurance companies to allow them to 'spread risk'. In reality, it involves back room dealings to facilitate all sorts of 'creative accountancy', in some cases moving losses onto 'off-balance' accounts. The IFSC became known as the Wild West of the European insurance industry because, as the *New York Times* put it:

> Regulators around the world have followed several trails of suspect financial transactions back to Ireland which more than a decade ago instituted accommodating tax and regulatory standards aimed at encouraging insurers to set up shop here.[38]

Third, the IFSC became one of the prime centres for hedge fund speculation in Europe with eight of the top hedge funds located there. Net assets of Irish domiciled funds totalled $1.241 trillion, and there were a total of 3,125 funds.[39] The IFSC provided them with an Irish address to promote their operations across Europe because, in reality, most were incorporated in the Cayman Islands and the British Virgin Islands, even more notorious tax havens than Ireland. US hedge fund companies dominated the IFSC and included Barclays/BGI, which had $164 billion in funds; Goldman Sachs ($99 billion); HSBC ($56 billion); BNY Mellon ($49 billion); and Russell Investment ($46 billion).[40] The funds were administered by companies like State Street International, which is headed by William Slattery, a former supervisor with the Central Bank, who was responsible for the IFSC. (Coincidently, the former Financial Regulator went on to the board of Merrill Lynch International Bank a year after he stepped

down from his state post.) Dublin's unique role as the main servicing centre for the Cayman Islands meant that it was involved
in the administration of a substantial number of these global
funds. In other words, Ireland was offered as a key platform to
facilitate global speculation.

As long as the philosophy of financial de-regulation was the
fashion of the day, the Irish state was able to benefit. It provided a
superficial show of regulation while giving every freedom that the
speculators demanded. Even when the IFSC was hit by a series of
scandals, the Irish state made little effort to clean up its act. In
2003, for example, the giant Italian food company Parmalat collapsed after it was revealed that it was faking its accounts through
an IFSC subsidiary. In 2005, the chief executive of the IFSC arm of
a re-insurance company, Cologne Re, pleaded guilty to creating a
deal to help cook the books for the giant insurance company,
AIG.[41] But the political elite simply turned a blind eye. The truth
was that 'financial services' was at the heart of the second phase
of Celtic Tiger and nothing would be done to upset the speculators who drove it forward.

The other main industry that characterised this phase of the
Celtic Tiger was the construction industry, and the reliance of the
Irish economy on this sector is well documented. The building
boom lasted over a thirteen-year period from 1993 to 2006 but the
real acceleration occurred after 2002. In the first phase of the Celtic
Tiger, house completions grew from 30,575 at the start of the
boom to 52,602 in 2001. Thereafter, the process of growth quick-
ened and 93,419 houses were completed in 2007. At this point, Ireland was building the equivalent of 21 housing units per 1,000 of
the population, compared with an average of 7 in the rest of
Western Europe. The only other country that experienced a housing boom of similar magnitude was Spain, but it still was only
building 15 units per 1,000. A similar boom occurred in commercial and retail property where even bigger profits could be made,
and soon hotels, office blocks and retail parks mushroomed across

the country. Construction accounted for 24 per cent of the output of the economy at one point.[42]

By 2007, at the height of the construction boom, there were 281,800 workers employed in construction, or 13.4 per cent of the workforce, twice the norm for most other EU countries. Ironically, many of these construction workers could not afford the price of houses in Dublin and elsewhere, and often travelled long distances to work, giving rise to a significant change in Irish eating habits. As Perry Share put it, the 'jumbo breakfast roll became the fuel for the Celtic cub'.[43]

The construction boom was accompanied by a celebration of the most naked values of jungle capitalism. Once the free market was let rip, it was supposed to enrich everyone. Although critical of the property boom, David McWilliams best captured the celebratory spirit of the time:

> Ireland is becoming the most middle class suburban nation in Europe and the most startling development in the past six years has been the rapid social mobility that the country is experiencing. The vast majority of us are climbing the social ladder not seen anywhere in Europe in forty years. We are now a middle class nation.[44]

The great irony was that the ladder had, literally, feet of clay because the Irish construction boom was like a gigantic pyramid scheme where builders tried to keep their asset values rising. The result was a huge over-production of housing. When the crash hit at the end of 2007, there were 266,332 unoccupied flats, holiday homes and houses, enough to house at least half a million people.[45] Many thousands are still on the housing waiting lists but they still cannot afford to buy these properties.

The construction boom exposed the fallacy of neoliberal economics on a spectacular scale. Contrary to all conventional laws about supply and demand, the more houses that were built, the more the prices increased. In 1991, the year which the Department of the Environment uses as its baseline year to measure price changes, the average new house cost €67,000. At the start of the boom in 1995, its price had risen almost exactly in line with inflation to €76,655, but after the Celtic Tiger started to roar it jumped repeatedly until 2007 when it stood at €331,947. In other words, house prices had risen by 480 per cent from the original baseline, even though house-building costs had grown by only 200 per cent.[46] Someone, it appeared, was making a hell of a lot of money.

Whenever money flies about, apologists will be found. The stockbroker economists who repeatedly cheered the boom pointed to Ireland's 'changing demographics' as the explanation. Growing numbers of migrants, a young population and a workforce with higher incomes had all helped fuel the boom. The implication was that the population had been bitten by a property bug and so had 'chosen' to push up prices.

There was, however, one glaring gap in this explanation. In an important article on the mechanisms of the Irish boom, Jerome Casey claimed that before the boom, building land represented 10 per cent to 15 per cent of Irish house prices.[47] By 2003, however, land accounted for 42.5 per cent of house prices nationwide and for 50 per cent of prices in Dublin. In the US and in Denmark, by contrast, building land accounted for 20 per cent of house prices while in Portugal it accounted for only 15 per cent. Land is an unusual commodity as its value can be directly affected by political factors. It has to be serviced by public authorities, and zoned for residential, agricultural or industrial uses. Crude attempts can be made to re-zone it by handing brown envelopes to buy local councillors, or more sophisticated systems can evolve to 'influence' decisions. The nexus between property and Irish local authority politics is vividly illustrated by the fact that an estimated 100 out of the 800 plus councillors elected in 2004 worked as estate agents or auctioneers.[48]

Where direct avenues to local political structures are not available, large construction companies invariably employed 'planning consultancy' companies like RPS. These progressed from engineering the physical environment to 'engineering' the required changes in public attitudes to facilitate 'development'. Through a host of techniques, such as controlled 'stake holder forums', they engage local community organisations in order to diffuse opposition and to allow the construction industry get its way.

The value of land can also be influenced by political developments at national level. Governments can impose land taxes or they can subject land to compulsory purchase orders. In 1973, for example, the Kenny report advocated that local authorities should have the power to acquire building land at use value prices, plus a 25 per cent premium, and even the economist Peter Bacon subsequently recommended a special Capital Gains Tax of 50 per cent on development land.[49] Yet the Irish state refused to take any of these measures, typically citing the argument that they could be construed as 'interference with market forces'.

This outlook gave great freedom to a small group of wealthy landowners to influence land prices. Casey gave an example of 25 individuals who controlled half of the land banks of the Fingal area of North Dublin, with zoning for more than 50,000 houses. The companies and individuals involved included:

- Bovale Developments: They were accused of obstructing the Flood Tribunal on planning and were later forced to make a tax settlement of €22.17 million to the Revenue Commissioners, the largest in Irish history. They were also regular attendees at the Fianna Fáil tent at the Galway races.

- Manor Park Homes: When Charles Haughey faced financial trouble after his appearance at the Moriarty tribunal, this company bought his house in Kinsealy for €45 million but allowed Haughey and his wife to remain there until they both died.

- McNamara Construction: This is owned by Bernard McNamara, a former Fianna Fáil councillor, who has been appointed to a number of state boards, including the Great Southern Ho-

tels Group, the National Roads Authority and the National
Gallery.

• Sean Mulryan: This is another prominent Fianna Fáil sup-
  porter and close associate of Charlie McCreevy. He made
  payments totalling €65,000 to the Fianna Fáil TD Liam Lawlor
  between 1994 and 1998.

The study of Fingal gave a glimpse of the real forces at work.
When examined in more detail, it becomes clear that the Irish construction boom was driven by a tight alliance between Fianna Fáil,
the bankers and the big builders. Each elements of the alliance
brought their own particular expertise to create an orgy of greed
that has led to a catastrophic fall.

The Bankers: The building boom could not have happened without frenetic lending by the banks. They bought money in the de-
regulated international markets, and channelled it back to Ireland
for property speculation. Until the introduction of the euro in 1999,
lending by Irish Banks was limited by the amount of savings de-
posited by companies and individuals. After entry to the eurozone,
however, Irish banks began to borrow vast sums to fund speculation at home and abroad. Between 1999 and 2008, the volume of
inter-bank borrowing and debt securities of Irish banks rose from
€31 billion to €150 billion.[50] In addition to this huge influx of funds,
the banks also channelled a high proportion of domestic deposits
back into property speculation, lending out 60 per cent of all the
deposits placed by Irish residents. By the end of the boom, the Irish
banks had lent out a vast fortune to builders and developers.[51]

The motivation was sheer greed. Driven by a desire to achieve
astronomical profits and bonuses for their chief executives, the
banks joined in the frenzied speculation with great gusto. Although their loan to deposit ratio was one of the highest for industrial countries, their confidence in Irish office blocks, 'credit
risk transfer products' and Spanish apartments knew no bounds.

Before the boom, the Irish banking system operated though a gentlemanly ethos where credit was restricted to people with a solid middle class career or commercial concerns. The change of direction came as Anglo Irish Bank led the way. At the start of the boom it accounted for only three per cent of the banking market but, by the end, it had risen to eighteen per cent of the market.[52] Morgan Kelly explains the trick:

> Anglo-Irish epitomised the Irish bubble economy. Its rise began a decade ago as the boom created a demand for houses and commercial property. As prices started to rise, banks made a miraculous discovery: the more they lent, the more prices rose; and the more prices rose, the more people wanted loans to get into the booming market. And the more loans that bankers made, the bigger the bonuses they could award themselves.[53]

Anglo Irish Bank had close connections with the Fianna Fáil party. Sean Fitzpatrick, the bank chairman, was a backroom advisor to Fianna Fáil, while Fintan Drury, who also served on its board, was so close to the party's current leader, Brian Cowen, that he was reputed to have 'walk-in privileges to the Taoiseach's office'.[54] Many of the bank's most prominent borrowers also had close Fianna Fáil connections. While Anglo Irish was lending out billions for large commercial property transactions, two of its board members, Sean Fitzpatrick and Lar Bradshaw, were backing a sub-prime business that targeted the vulnerable.[55] But where Anglo forged a path, others quickly followed.

It would be wrong, however, to assume that there was a distinct class of financiers who created the bubble. Those responsible were part of an interlocking chain that stretched right across the heart of Irish capitalism. Sean Fitzpatrick, the chair of Anglo Irish Bank, was a director of Greencore and Smurfit Kappa; Donal O'Connor, who succeeded him as director, was on the board of Elan and Readymix; Ned O'Sullivan, another director of Anglo

Irish, was also a director of McInerney; Dermot Gleeson, the chair of Allied Irish Bank, was also a director of Independent News and Media; David Dilger, a director of Bank of Ireland, used to be the chief executive of Greencore, and so on. The network that ran the banks had tentacles that stretched deep into Irish industry.

Fianna Fáil: The party's links with the construction industry has traditionally run deep. The links began with companies such as Cement Roadstone Holdings, the giant multi-national that has since risen to become a world player. The former Fianna Fáil Taoiseach, Sean Lemass, was its first chairman, and Des Traynor, who was later described as the 'bag man' for Lemass's son-in-law, Charles Haughey, was also a chair of CRH. Traynor even organised the Ansbacher account from the company's office and more than half of the board of directors of CRH contributed to the fund. Yet an official investigation found no link between the company and the Ansbacher account.

Fianna Fáil also received substantial funds from the biggest builders, who paraded themselves openly at the Fianna Fáil tent at the Galway races, where patrons paid €4,000 a table. Most of the big builders such as Sean Mulryan, Bernard McNamara, Michael Bailey, Padraig Rhatigan, Sean Dunne, Johnny Rohan and Pascal Taggart have all attended the tent. Further down the pecking order at local level, Fianna Fáil candidates receive support from a host of small builders.

The relationship between the party and the big builders is entirely symbiotic. In government, Fianna Fáil introduced a host of measures which stimulated the property boom. Some developed in an ad hoc manner as a way to prolong the Celtic Tiger, but, equally, Fianna Fáil gained votes and party funds while the construction boom lasted. Some of the key measures supported by the party included:

- The abolition of the residential property tax in 1997. Instead of adjusting the tax to take account of rising property prices, and to garner more revenue from expensive property, the tax was simply abolished.

- The reduction of the Capital Gains Tax from 40 per cent to 20 per cent – including on second homes. This facilitated the investor market in buying and selling houses for huge profits.

- The encouragement of the use of the Section 23 tax breaks which provided tax relief on construction or refurbishment of apartments. This was originally introduced in 1981 but was not used to great effect until the 1990s. It allows developers to write off rental income on the other Irish properties they own and thus effectively subsidise their purchase.

- The Seaside Resort Scheme (or to give it its official title, The Pilot Relief Scheme for the Renewal and Improvement of Certain Resort Areas) which allowed investors to offset building costs against other income.

- A student accommodation relief scheme introduced in the Finance Act of 1999. This was similar to the Section 23 scheme.

The combined effect of these tax relief measures was to create a new layer of property investors, many of whom became landlords. Table 1.5 shows that after 2001, first time buyers fell as a proportion of the overall market, while the percentage of the 'other' category grew. The 'other' category consisted mainly of landlords and holiday home owners. This layer of society stoked up the property boom and turned property into a speculative item rather than one which served a real need for accommodation.

Fianna Fáil's policies accelerated the property boom in other significant ways aside from tax relief. Their wider agenda of cutting back on public services led to a reduction of spending on local authority housing, when compared to the levels of economic growth. Between 1991 and 2002, the number of local authority houses fell from 10 per cent of the housing completions to 6 per cent. This forced more people into the private rented sector but Fianna Fáil refused to implement any form of rent control, deeming it to be an interference in the market. As rents rose during the boom years, young workers were encouraged to 'get their foot on the property ladder' with 30 or even 40 year mortgages. Monthly mortgage repayments did not appear, at the time, to be much higher than rent because of the low interest rates. And so they were told to 'take the plunge'.

Table 1.5: Percentage of First Time and 'Other' Buyers of Housing Units

	Whole Country		Dublin	
	First Time Buyers	Others	First Times Buyers	Others
2001	63	37	66	34
2004	48	52	48	52
2007	34	66	35	66

Source: Department of Environment, Heritage and Local Government Database Ownership Status of Borrowers.

Fianna Fáil also stoked up the property boom by encouraging the sell-off of state land to private developers. The former Eastern Regional Health Authority sold off four of its sites in Dublin for €106 million, even though internal documents from the agency reported that they were valued at €576 million.[56] CIE was told to sell-off valuable land when its rail freight division was systematically closed down to make way for road haulage. The chief beneficiaries were property developers who undertook large office projects or apartment complexes on these sites.

A further stimulus for the construction boom came from the National Roads Authority. Successive boards of directors included key figures from the Construction Industry Federation and directors of building and engineering firms. Coincidently, the NRA has a particularly poor record on its projected costings. In November 1999, for example, it was estimated that €6 billion would be spent on improving the national road network, but three years later this had risen to €16 billion.[57] Large construction companies, and farmers who owned land on planned routes, were among the principal beneficiaries of these cost overruns.

The political nexus that linked the state to the fortunes made in construction is best symbolised by the career of one of Fianna Fáil's allies, Tom Parlon. As the leader of the Irish Farmers Association, Parlon managed to do a deal with the NRA which awarded farmers €4.6 billion in compensation for land used by the road network. Later, as a Progressive Democrat minister who was responsible for the Office of Public Works, Parlon pushed through a de-centralisation policy that involved the purchase and rent of new office blocks which cost the state an estimated €900 million.[58] Finally, after leaving politics, he re-appeared as the boss of the Construction Industry Federation to lobby Finance Minister Brian Lenihan to retain dearer 'cost plus' contracts, rather than the more stringent 'better value' contracts, for a new raft of construction projects.[59] His scaling of boundaries between state and private interests was symbolic of a wider philosophy which identified profit with good citizenship.

The Builders: The principal beneficiaries of the extraordinary boom were a very small group of builders. Seventeen of the top fifty people in the Sunday Times Rich List of 2009 are involved in either property or construction and are by far the largest category.[60] Many of them put on the most ostentatious displays of wealth, in a phenomenon that the US sociologist Thorstein Veblen labelled as 'conspicuous consumption'.[61]

Owning a set of 'blades' – a helicopter – was often the norm for the building elite. Others went one step further and purchased their own private jets, and several took out private boxes at the Lans-

downe Rugby stadium at a cost of €475,000 for five years. Bernard
McNamara set the trend in building trophy mansions when he demolished the old Japanese Embassy to make way for a 15,000+
square foot edifice on Ailesbury Road, complete with swimming
pool and private dance hall. Another builder, Derek Quinlan of
Quinlan Private, paid €25 million for two large houses in Shrews-
bury Road. He then demolished them to make way for a palatial
mansion consisting of seven enormous bedrooms, an indoor
swimming pool, a gym, massage room and two wine cellars, all
laid out over four floors.[62]

The wealthiest among them made a fortune in Ireland and then
began to invest in commercial property abroad. In 2007, Irish investment accounted for the second highest proportion of European
property with €14 billion being invested. Contrary to claims that
their wealth has been washed away in the crash, many of these
people still control valuable real estate outside Ireland. Despite the
mythology about being entrepreneurial 'risk-takers', the Irish rich
prefer the safe ground of property because they know from experience that it can be laced with good political connections.

But, it will be claimed, 'they at least provided jobs'. In an up-
side down world, those who extract wealth are portrayed as bene-
factors rather than exploiters of labour. Yet a closer examination
of what actually occurred on building sites raises questions about
their apparent generosity. During the boom years, the number of
directly employed workers fell as a proportion of the workforce,
and by 2007 there were 72,000 people registered as 'self-
employed' in the industry, accounting for just over a quarter. The
Construction Industry Federation appears to have deliberately
promoted employment agencies and forced workers on to a bogus
self-employment status. As one union activist informed a SIPTU
conference, 'you could just have a bucket and shovel and still be
registered as a sole trader'.[63] Through these mechanisms, many
workers were forced to sign away their rights to social protection
and, particularly, pension cover. A report by the pensions con-

sultant, Mercer, stated quite bluntly that 'in our view many of these operatives are not self-employed in the accepted sense of the term'.[64] It noted that self-employment was the main reason why pension coverage had been reduced in the industry.

The Celtic Tiger, therefore, arose from a fortuitous set of circumstances when US corporations sought a home inside EU tariff barriers. Ireland pulled off a great stroke of transforming itself into a tax haven, becoming one of the main recipients of that investment. The trick worked for a comparatively short period and allowed the political elite to inculcate a version of neoliberalism which was summed up in the phrase 'jobs at any price'.

But while neoliberalism gained a temporary victory, it left a destructive legacy as the boom was squandered because of an ideological opposition to channelling investment into the public services. Instead, the state did everything to give tax breaks to private investors to allow them to enrich themselves. They hoped that this would create a trickle down effect that would keep the population content. So they ran down the health service to allow private investors establish co-located private hospitals with huge tax breaks. They held back investment from some of the poorest flat complexes in Dublin and, instead, gave out Public Private Partnership contracts to help the balance sheets of wealthy builders. The most lasting legacy of the Celtic Tiger is probably an improved road network and a host of private apartment complexes which contain many unoccupied units.

When the boom faltered in 2002, the political elite could have changed direction but, instead, they accelerated in the same way they were going. Finance and construction became the two vehicles for prolonging the boom. A distorted economy ran for a few more years on the lethal and combustible fuel of speculation. The elite were cheered on by a host of economic experts who celebrated statistics of growth, and took these as evidence for their own dogmatic beliefs that deregulation and free market fundamentalism worked wonders. Today, the wreckage of the Celtic

Tiger is strewn everywhere but the apologists make no effort to examine an economic philosophy which was promoted for over 20 years. In the next chapter, we will look at the failures of neoliberalism, the party line of the state bureaucracy, here and elsewhere, until the current crash.

Endnotes

---

[1] 'Follow the Leapin' Leprechaun', *New York Times*, 1 July 2005.

[2] B. Powell, 'Economic Freedom and Growth: The case of the Celtic Tiger', *Cato Journal*, Vol. 22 No. 3 (2003) pp. 431-448.

[3] A. Eiras, 'The United States is no longer the champion of Economic Freedom', *Heritage Foundation* Website www.heritage.org/research/tradeandforignaid/bg1781.cfm

[4] N. Vardy, Investing in Ireland: The Surprising Roar of the Celtic Tiger www.theglobalguru.com/article.php?id=71

[5] Eurostat, *Structures of the Taxation Systems in the European Union* (Luxembourg: Office of Official Publications of the European Communities, 2004)

[6] M.A. Wren, *Unhealthy State: Anatomy of a Sick Society* (Dublin: New Island, 2003) p. 146.

[7] *Working to Our Advantage: A National Workplace Strategy: Report on Forum of Workplace of the Future* (Dublin: Centre for Partnership Performance, 2005) p. 62.

[8] ' ASTI Survey reveals inadequate resources and facilities for teaching Science at Second Level' http://www.asti.ie/pr2006/ prapr06.htm#science

[9] Eurostat, *Europe in Figures: Eurostat yearbook 2005* (Luxembourg: Office of Official Publications of European Commission. 2005), p. 138.

[10] Pensions Board, *National Pensions Review* (Dublin: Pensions Board, 2005), p. 38.

[11] Dail Debates, Vol. 25, Col. 478, 12 July 1928.

[12] K. Allen, *Fianna Fáil and Irish Labour* (London: Pluto Press, 1997), Ch. 1.

[13] *Report of Tribunal of Inquiry (Dunnes Payments), McCracken Tribunal* (Dublin: Stationery Office, 1997), p. 58.

[14] P. Ginsborg, *Italy and Its Discontents* (London: Allen Lane, 2002).

[15] P. Robb, *Midnight in Sicily* (London: Vintage, 2003).

[16] M. Marsh, 'Party identification in Ireland: An insecure anchor for a floating party system', *Electoral Studies*, Vol. 25, No. 3 (2006), pp. 489-508.

[17] R. Barrell and N. Pain, 'The Growth of Foreign Investment in Europe', *National Institute Economic Review*, no 160 (1997), p. 63.

[18] See Revenue Commissioners Press Release, 'Signature of New Tax Convention between Ireland and the US', 28 July 1997.

[19] M. O'Sullivan, 'Data Shows Dramatic Shift of Profits to Tax Havens', *Tax Notes*, 13 September 2004

[20] IDA, *Annual Report 1998* (Dublin, IDA, 1998), p.12.

[21] F. Barry, J. Bradley and E. O Malley, 'Indigenous and Foreign Industry: Characteristics and Performance' in F. Barry (ed) *Understanding Ireland's Economic Growth* (Basingstoke, Macmillan, 1999) p. 46.

[22] M. Cassidy, 'Productivity in Ireland: Trends and Issues', *Central Bank Quarterly Bulletin*, Spring 2004, pp. 83-105.

[23] T. Dobbins, 'Irish industrial relations system no longer voluntarist', *Industrial Relations News*, No.10, 3 March 2005.

[24] P. Tansey, *Productivity: Ireland's Economic Imperative: A study of Ireland's productivity performance and the implications for Ireland's future economic success* (Dublin: Microsoft 2005), Tables 20 and 21.

[25] J. Power, *How Robust is Ireland's Foreign Direct Investment Model* (Dublin: Friends First 2008) p. 14.

[26] D. McKitterick, 'Ireland's Second Biggest Employer Defects to Poland', *Independent*, 9 January 2009.

[27] T. Palley, *Financialization: What it is and Why it Matters* (Political Economic Research Institute, University of Massachusetts, Amherst, 2007); G. Epstein, *Financialization and World Economy* (London: Edward Elgar, 2006).

[28] R. Boyer, 'Is finance-led growth regime a viable alternative to Fordism? A preliminary analysis', *Economy and Society*, Vol. 29, No. 1, 2000, pp. 111-145.

[29] S. Becker, 'Irish patient has to swallow the bitter medicine of correcting past exuberance', Deutsche Bank Research, 10 March 2009.

[30] Ibid.

[31] Central Bank and Financial Services Authority of Ireland, *Financial Stability Report 2007* p. 5.

[32] P. Neary, A Principles Approach to Regulation. Address to PAI Regulation Ireland Conference, 16 July 2007.

[33] Regulating Better: Government White paper setting out six principles of regulation (Dublin: Stationary Office, 2004) pp. 20-21.

[34] Ibid.

[35] IDA, The IFSC. Package of material sent to author.

[36] Ibid.

[37] Financial Services Ireland, The Financial Services Industry in Ireland: Power Point Presentation 2006 on IBEC website.

[38] B. Lavery and T. O'Brien, 'Insurers' Trail leads to Dublin', *New York Times*, 1 April 2005.

[39] 'Fund Industry to hit $2 trillion mark', *Sunday Business Post*, 9 November 2008.

[40] Ibid.

[41] 'F. O'Toole, 'We ignored the warnings about low regulation', *Irish Times*, 17 February 2009.

[42] Goodbody Stockbrokers, *Irish Construction Economics* (Dublin: Goodbody, 2006) p. 2.

[43] P. Share, 'Jumbo Breakfast Roll' in M. Corcoran and P. Share (eds.) *Belongings: A Sociological Chronicle 2005-2006* (Dublin: IPA 2008).

[44] D. McWilliams, *The Pope's Children: Ireland's New Elite* (Dublin: Gill and MacMillan, 2005) p. 123.

[45] J. Brennan and J Reilly, 'Over 266,000 homes lies vacant nationwide', *Irish Independent*, 23 December 2007.

[46] Department of Environment, Heritage and Local Government Housing Statistics Data Base: Indices for House Prices, Mortgage Interest Rates, Earnings, House Building Costs and Consumer Prices.

[47] Jerome Casey & Co. 'An Analysis of Economic and Marketing Influences on the Construction Industry', *Building Industry Bulletin*, July 2003.

[48] F. McDonald. *The Builders* (Dublin: Penguin, 2008) p. 6.

[49] P. Bacon, *An Economic Assessment of House Price Developments* (Dublin: Stationary Office, 1998) p. 89.

[50] 'ECB move only way to end banks Catch-22', *Irish Independent*, 2 November 2008.

[51] 'Bailout inept and potentially dangerous', *Irish Times*, 2 October 2008.

[52] P. Honohan and P. Lane, Ireland in Crisis. 28 February 2009 http://www.irisheconomy.ie/index.php/2009/02/28/vox-ireland-in-crisis/

[53] 'Better to incinerate €1.5 billion than squander it on Anglo Irish Bank', *Irish Times*, 23 December 2008.

[54] 'Government on a tight rope', *Sunday Business Post*, 22 February 2009.

[55] 'Irish bankers fell into sub-prime trap'. *Sunday Business Pos* , 20 July 2008/

[56] 'State land sold off at one fifth of its value'. *Village Magazine.* 18 January 2007/

[57] Comptroller and Auditor General, *National Roads Authority Improvement Programme*, April 2004, p. 8.

[58] 'Decentralisation to cost 900 million', *Sunday Business Post*, 17 October 2004.

[59] 'Parlon wins U Turn with €150m deal for builders', *Irish Independent*, 6 October 2008.

[60] *Sunday Times* Rich List 2009 http://business.timesonline.co.uk/richlist-app/index.php?l=29&pageID=2

[61] T. Veblen, *The Leisure Class* (Penguin, Harmondsworth, 1994).

[62] McDonald, *The Builders*, p. 15.

[63] Paul Hansard speaking at SIPTU Conference 2007.

[64] Mercer, *Review of Construction Federation Operatives Pension Scheme*, (Dublin: Mercer, 2005) p. 5.

2

THE FAILURE OF NEOLIBERALISM

MOST THOUGHT IT WOULD NEVER happen again. The Wall Street Crash of 1929 was supposed to belong to the history books. The following Depression was said to be the stuff of novels and films. But here we are; it is starting all over again. By the end of 2009, the International Labour Organisation estimates 50 million people will be unemployed because of the current global economic crisis. A further 200 million will join the 'working poor' who earn less than €2 a day.[1] This is social suffering on a vast scale, and it is causing panic in elite circles. For example, the US Director of National Intelligence, Denis Blair, has predicted that social instability will become the greatest threat to the United States – even greater than 'terrorism'.[2]

And, of course, the elite has every reason to feel afraid. In Iceland and Latvia, governments have been driven out of office by outbursts of popular anger. In Greece, unemployed youth rose up against police repression and poverty wages. In Martinique and Guadeloupe, a six-week general strike forced politicians to raise the minimum wage. These victories in France's 'overseas departments' have inspired three million French workers to take part in two general strikes. A wave of protest has even engulfed China as millions of migrants who moved from the countryside have been laid off and languish without jobs in the cities. In the Pearl River Delta, which has become the workshop of the world, pitched battles have been fought between police and striking workers.[3]

Before getting to grips with the underlying ideas about the crisis we face, it is worth noting that the current situation facing the global economy has three main dimensions.

FINANCIAL

The most obvious dimension is the near collapse of the global financial system. The epicentre of all the trouble was the US 'subprime' market, in which banks pushed credit on poor households who were enticed to buy 'teaser' mortgages that started off with low repayments, and then rose steeply. These mortgage obligations were 'sliced and diced' and sold off to the global finance industry. And so, as the sub-prime market unravelled, other 'financial instruments', or exotic forms of speculation, were drawn into the collapse. Now, the world's finance system is holding a vast amount of 'toxic debt' – worthless paper that will never be repaid.

One example is the giant insurance company, AIG, which made a loss of $62 billion in the last quarter of 2008, the largest in US corporate history. This is the equivalent of $27 million for every single hour – or, on an annual basis, the size of the economy of a modest African country, such as Libya. On a global level, it is estimated that the collapse of financial assets will mean a write down of $4.1 trillion.[4]

MAIN STREET

The crisis has spread from Wall Street to Main Street, i.e. into the heart of the manufacturing and services economy. Now there is not just a 'credit crunch' but also a depression that has started a vicious cycle of stagnant investment, growing unemployment and a collapse in markets. One clear sign is the unprecedented slump in trade. In November 2008, global trade in goods and services had fallen by 45 per cent on the previous year – a figure not even seen during the great depression.[5] The Baltic Dry Index, which measures the movement of freight in commodities like iron ore and grain, dropped by 95 per cent last year, and remained at zero in early 2009.[6] This is already having a devastating effect on many developing countries that were advised to focus on exporting rather than their home markets.

GEOPOLITICAL CRISIS?

Since the 1990s, the world economy has been sustained by a symbiotic relationship between China and the US. China rose to become a major exporter to the US, a situation symbolised by the dominance of Wal-Mart, which imports vast quantities of cheap Chinese-made goods. This trade gave the Chinese government a huge surplus which they stored by buying US bonds. Even before the current depression, this allowed the US to run up huge debts. Despite the weakness of the US economy, it was also able to maintain the dollar at a relatively high level and sustain its position as the pre-eminent global currency. These mechanisms allowed the US ruling class to cream off a slice of the world's surplus through the financial system and bankroll a huge military machine which otherwise would have to be curtailed.

However, the current crisis puts the US–Chinese relationship under great strain. As export opportunities slow down, the Chinese authorities have tried to ward off social unrest by embarking on a huge stimulus programme. If this leads to a withdrawal of funds from the US, it would have devastating consequences because it would then be harder for the US government to sustain its multi-billion rescue package. The Chinese government has already begun to attack the dollar's privileged role as a reserve currency in the global financial order. The economic crisis has, therefore, laid the basis for an even deeper geopolitical crisis that can set the US and China on a collision course.

RISK-TAKERS

Even before this develops, the economic crisis has exposed rulers in ways that has not been seen since the Gorbachev era of *glasnost* in the old USSR in the late 1980s. For decades, the people of Russia were told to obey the orders of the Politburo of the Communist Party and to honour the legacy of party dictators. But as the old model of state control became inefficient, the political language suddenly changed, and the population were told to accept glasnost or 'openness' and market mechanisms. Although the dramatic shift in ideological discourse was led by the Communist Party leader, Gorbachev, it proved fatal for that party. The French writer, Alexis de Tocqueville, explains why:

> Experience suggests that the most dangerous moment for an evil government is usually when it begins to reform itself.... The sufferings that are endured patiently, as being inevitable, become intolerable the moment it appears that there might be an escape. Reform then only serves to reveal more clearly what still remains oppressive and now all the more unbearable.[7]

A similar change in outlook is presently occurring in Western capitalism. For more than thirty years, people were subjected to a political language that worshipped 'entrepreneurs' and 'entrepreneurship'. Capitalists re-branded themselves as 'innovators' – the source of dynamism in modern economies whose audacity, brilliance and, above all, ability to take risks would generate wealth for all.

And it was this risk-taking which became the principal justification for inequalities. Consider for a moment the possible alternatives by asking: Why is it right that three billionaires – Warren Buffet, Bill Gates and Sam Walton – can share between them more wealth than the entire people of sub-Saharan Africa?

Of course, if one were of a particular religious persuasion, one might suggest that this is simply how God designed the world, and so it just has to be accepted. This type of justification was used in pre-capitalist societies to explain differences between peasants and aristocrats. But few people today would accept that God chose a particular family to be His representatives on earth and that they deserve a vast fortune while others starve.

Another possible justification might be based on merit. So it might be claimed that Buffet, Gates and Walton have worked so hard that they rose to the top through the fruits of their energy, initiative and thrift. In Victorian England, this was a popular explanation for the difference between employers such as Josiah Wedgwood and his workforce. But even if we concede the dubious case about merit, the sheer scale of the inequality today would lead to a further question: Do the meritorious really deserve so much?

Rather than religion or merit, then, risk-taking has become the main justification for differences in wealth. Risk-takers are said to gamble all they own just to find new paths of economic development for society. They only engage in these risks because there are such great rewards. They need, therefore, to be 'incentivised' and, as a consequence, 'the markets' need full freedom to back these robust individuals when they show signs of success. Inequality and the relentless search for 'shareholder value' is, therefore, a condition for wealth creation.

Today, this mythology has been shattered. Far from capitalists being independent wealth creators, it is now clear just how quickly they will turn up with a begging bowl at the door of the government when in difficulty. The US government's multi-billion dollar bail out of its finance houses destroyed forever the argument about risk-taking. And, ironically, some advocates for the risk-takers have switched to become the most brazen supporters of corporate welfare. In 2006, for example, *Business Week* ran a cover story under the headline 'Mr Risk Goes to Washington' about the appointment of Henry Paulson as US Treasury Secretary. Paulson was the former Chief Executive of Goldman Sachs, a corporation that spearheaded the growth of speculation and privatisation. The magazine claimed that 'Hank Paulson's profound understanding of risk and reward makes him the perfect pick for the Treasury'.[8] But soon after settling in to office, Paulson was dispensing over €700 billion to the banks. 'Mr Risk' had become 'Mr Hand-out'.

And the sheer scale of the hand-outs to the super-rich is nothing if not obscene. Each night 850 million people in the world go to bed hungry. Yet, if the original $700 billion cheque Paulson wrote to the banks had gone to the starving, rather than to the bankers, hunger would be wiped out. If $1 trillion of the huge sums which have been written down had been used to alleviate suffering, then two billion of the world's six billion people could be immediately lifted out of chronic poverty. Obviously, the 'risk-taking' bankers are deemed more important to the future of the planet than millions of potentially productive workers.

NEOLIBERALS

Crucially, however, all of this is only the tip of the ideological crisis that faces advocates of capitalism. The whole façade of what we can call 'neoliberalism' has been cracked by the current crisis. In the 1980s, neoliberalism became the official dogma of global elites. Neoliberal orthodoxy calls for shrinking the state, maintaining balanced budgets and supporting market forces. Public enterprises were deemed inefficient and in need of privatisation. Citizens with social rights henceforth became customers who could choose, provided only that they paid for public services. Controls on the movement of capital were abolished and taxes on profit and wealth were cut. Deregulation was encouraged, particularly of the financial sector. According to Alan Greenspan, the former Chair of the US Federal Reserve and once a follower of the libertarian Ayn Rand, government regulation was damaging because it undercut financial innovation and risk-taking. Offshore banking and exotic financial engineering became the order of the day.

One noteworthy contemporary advocate of the new doctrine is the *New York Times* columnist, Thomas Friedman, whose book, *The Lexus and the Olive Tree* has sold all over the world. He suggested that every country had to fit into the 'golden straightjacket' of complying with markets. In this brave new world:

> Political choices get reduced to Pepsi or Coke – to slight nuances of taste, slight nuances of policy, slight alterations of design to account for local traditions, some loosening here and there, but never any major deviation from the core golden rules.... (But) the tighter you wear it, the more gold it produces and the more padding you can then put into it for your society.[9]

Neoliberal dogmas never had much resonance before the mid-1970s. Until then, the dominant, Keynesian, view was that the market should be managed by the state through controls on capital movement, interest rate adjustments and counter-cyclical spending to stimulate economies in danger of recession. Neoliberalism was seen as an 'extremist' doctrine held by only a few right wing fanatics. Indeed, in 1962, when Milton Friedman, one of the intellectual fathers of neoliberalism, published *Capitalism and Freedom,* he felt he was part 'of a small beleaguered minority regarded as eccentrics by the great majority of our fellow intellectuals'![10] Just twenty years later, however, the neoliberal vision dominated the mindsets of the global elites.

Hayek's Vision

The neoliberal doctrine had originally been pushed by Frederick Hayek. He was an economist who claimed that only the market could provide 'a system for the utilization of knowledge, which no one can possess as a whole'.[11] As long as there was no interference from the state, the market would send out price signals that indicated where investment was needed, and where there was an abundance or scarcity of goods. Interference came from political structures which enabled people to impose some of their demands on blind market forces. Hayek's neoliberalism, therefore, targeted any form of robust democratic input as a threat to the market.

In 1944, he published his classic text, *The Road to Serfdom*, which argued that Nazism was an outgrowth of 'collectivism'. By that he meant a tendency towards greater state control, which, he claimed, both Keynes and Marx had advocated. During the Cold War, a small number of economists read this book, which was mainly seen as an attack on 'communism'. But after the oil crisis of 1973, when Keynesianism was undermined by its inability to tackle the subsequent global recession, the neoliberal argument against interference in the market found a new audience.

Hayek was quite open about his distrust of democracy. In *Law, Legislation and Liberty* he stated that:

> The predominant model of liberal democratic institution, in which the same representative body lays down the rules of just conduct and directs government, necessarily leads to a gradual transformation of the spontaneous order of a free society into a totalitarian system conducted in the service of some coalition of organised interests.[12]

Hayek's aim was to reduce the 'politicisation' of society in order to keep public action to a minimum. His key concern was to limit the scope of governmental decision-making through a constitution and restrict its financial powers.[13] In this way the 'spontaneous order' of the market could be given free reign.

His followers advocated a number of devices to restrict popular input into the workings of the economy. These included: laws to ensure that budgets were balanced; restrictions on government borrowing, such as those exemplified in the EU Growth and Stability pact; the creation of an 'independent' central bank; and rules which restricted the state from favouring public concerns over private companies.

Hayek formed a close connection with the University of Chicago, which eventually became the intellectual powerhouse of neoliberalism. One of the central tenets of the 'Chicago School' was Eugene Fama's 'efficient markets hypothesis'. This claimed that a market, which provides all available information, is efficient and will correct itself continuously.[14] This thesis led the neoliberals to emphasise a certain form of 'transparency' because they thought that any group which had a monopolistic control of information relevant to price formation would distort the market. Once this transparency was in place, it was assumed that prolonged market disruptions would be rare and that there would be no need for 'burdensome regulations' that only led to 'financial repression'.

The neoliberals did not assume that markets were a natural phenomenon that reflected a human propensity to truck and barter, as Adam Smith had thought. When Smith was writing, monopolies barely existed, and there was little state intervention. But this was at the start of industrial capitalism, before the birth of the 'collectivist ethos', which Hayek loathed.

Hayek's peculiar perspective – which was transmitted to the Chicago school – was to confront the 'collectivist tide' from a minority position. Neoliberals, therefore, saw themselves continually fighting entrenched elites to save the market – even when they themselves had become the entrenched elite. This explains why they placed such great emphasis on the 'battle of ideas' and formed 'think tanks' to influence public opinion. Foundations funded by corporations such as Coors or Exxon Mobil were created to support a vast network of inter-linked neoliberal think tanks in many countries. Some of these, such as the Heritage Foundation, the Cato Institute or the American Enterprise Institute, purported to present neutral academic research, which was then reported in the popular press. In reality, they all just transmitted an interpretation of the world for neoliberal advocates on a daily basis. And underneath the main think tanks lay an even larger network, 'perhaps the most potent, independent institutionalised apparatus ever assembled in a democracy to promote one belief system.'[15]

Neoliberals also captured the 'commanding heights' of key global institutions such as the IMF, the World Bank and the OECD. The OECD used its considerable institutional power to promote the neoliberal agenda in the industrialised countries. Each year, for example, around 60,000 senior civil servants and politicians attended meetings in its Chateau de la Muette offices in Paris, where they sometimes engaged in 'consensus building through peer pressure'.[16]

Joseph Stiglitz, the former Chief Economist and Senior Vice President of the World Bank, has provided a detailed critique on how neoliberal ideas were pushed via the World Bank and the IMF, which worked together to impose neoliberal policies on developing countries. He noted that the IMF was not particularly interested in hearing the thoughts of its 'client countries' because it saw itself as:

> ... the font of wisdom, the purveyor of orthodoxy too subtle to be grasped by those in the developing world. The message conveyed was all too clear: in the best cases there was a member of an elite – a minister of finance or the head of a central bank – with whom the Fund might have a meaningful dialogue. Outside this circle, there was little point even trying to talk.[17]

The neoliberals were therefore able to work through powerful institutions to impose their views on the world. They were supported by a corporate media owned by figures such as Rupert Murdoch and Tony O'Reilly who blared out the message daily through their press. Two key rhetorical devices were used to promote the message.

One was to invert the class pyramid so that business people and supporters of market forces became the victims of a Keynesian intelligentsia. Neoliberals portrayed themselves as 'outsiders' fighting against the established 'egg head' elite. The tabloid press raged against a variety of targets, such as funding for the arts, resources allocated to asylum seekers, and social welfare recipients – while they championed business people who were held back by 'red tape'. Market fundamentalists, who required more intellectual ammunition to support this rage, referred to the Director's Law, named after Aaron Director, one of the earliest participants of Hayek's first think tank, the Mont Pelerin Society. This 'law' purported to show that public expenditure is carried out for the benefit of the 'middle class', and is financed by taxes that penalise both the rich and the poor.[18] In this imagery, rich people like Bill Gates become the philanthropists who care for Africa's poor, while liberal do-gooders increase taxes to penalise both entrepreneurs and decent hard working people.

The second rhetorical device was to present pro-market changes as an inevitable sign of 'modernisation'. The French sociologist Pierre Bourdieu has argued that neoliberals used the term globalisation as a 'myth' to change social behaviour. Behind the myth were 'market forces' which had no names but which were akin to powerful spirits that controlled our lives. Human agency was reduced to zero as we had no choice but to comply with the signals they sent. Although it represented a conservative reaction that sought a return to the pure market capitalism of Adam Smith's day, neoliberalism also appealed to modernity and reason. As Bourdieu pointed out:

> It is not like in other times a question of evoking an idealized past by the exaltation of blood and soil – agrarian and archaic themes. This new type of conservative revolution appeals to progress, reason, and science (economics, in this event) to justify restoration and seeks in this

way to dispatch progressive thought and action to an archaic past.[19]

Opponents of neoliberal measures were projected as backward, parochial and unable to comprehend the complexities of modernisation. They hankered after a distant past, and could not let go of their desire for a 'nanny' state. They just did not understand the 'new realities'. The fashionable sociologist Ulrick Beck explained the failure to grow up and face the new world. In a rather condescending metaphor, he wrote that:

> During the first age of modernity, capital, labour and state played at making sand cakes in the sandpit (a sandpit limited and organised in terms of the nation state) and during this game each side tried to knock the other's sand cake off the spade in accordance with the rules of institutionalised conflict. Now suddenly business was given a present of a mechanical digger and is emptying the whole sandpit. The trade unions and the politicians, who have been left out of the new game, have gone off in a huff and are crying for mummy.[20]

THE END OF THE ROAD?

Today, this whole edifice is in tatters, as neoliberals recant and proclaim themselves converts to regulation. When Alan Greenspan appeared before the House Oversight Committee of the US Senate in 2008 to discuss the nation's economic crisis, he candidly admitted that he was in a 'state of shocked disbelief' and acknowledged that there was 'a flaw in the model that defines how the world works'.[21]

Just six years before, he had argued: 'If risk is properly dispersed, shocks to the overall economic system will be better absorbed and less likely to create cascading failures that could threaten financial stability.'[22]

Before leaving office, George Bush had to carry out more na-
tionalisation than any previous US President since the 1930s. Yet
Bush had energised his supporters by continually attacking 'Big
Government'.

In Britain, the Chair of the Financial Services Authority issued
a report that lambasted the philosophy of self-regulating markets.
According to Lord Turner:

> The financial crisis has challenged the intellectual as-
> sumptions on which previous regulatory approaches
> were largely built, and in particular the theory of rational
> and self-correcting markets. Much financial innovation
> has proved of little value, and market discipline of indi-
> vidual bank strategies has often proved ineffective.[23]

In Ireland, the same chorus of recanting is also underway, but
in far more muted tones. Economists who praised the regime of
deregulation in the past now pour scorn on the cosy relationship
between the official regulators and the banks. Virtually all
economists support state intervention to guarantee the banks –
even those who once loudly proclaimed their opposition to any
subsidies that might distort the free market. They are virtually
unanimous in suggesting that the future lies with a 'regular and
regulated capitalism' – a term coined by the French President,
Nicholas Sarkozy.

However, while neoliberalism has been exposed as a fraudu-
lent intellectual doctrine, the original impetus that gave rise to it is
by no means dead. The real purpose of the doctrine was to give an
intellectual cover to an attempt by the world's rulers to restore the
balance of class power after the 1960s revolt. In particular, they
wanted to weaken union power, and cut the social wage given to
workers through the public services. The aim was to cut taxes and
abolish any redistributive element in the tax code. But to do so the
wealthy needed a much larger support base of advocates in the
wider society. By offering a rigorous alternative to the left, neolib-

eralism emerged as the most coherent intellectual paradigm for defenders of the system. It energised a host of economics graduates and MBAs, and gave them zeal to promote market fundamentalism.

Its very utopian image – that capitalism is based on pure competition – was an asset for ideologists. Apologists for inequality do not need to concern themselves with the real mechanisms by which money assumes a dictatorial power. They simply need a logic based on abstract assumptions about how capitalism works and a moral charge that came with rhetoric about 'freedom and choice'.

The intellectual role that neoliberalism played for capitalism was akin to that played by Max Weber in the early twentieth century. At the time, Marxism was popular in Germany and many were familiar with Marx's account of primitive accumulation. According to Marx, the origins of capitalism depended on a host of factors – slavery, the expropriation of church property, the expulsion of the peasantry from common land – to accumulate its initial capital. However, in his classic book, *The Protestant Ethic and the Spirit of Capitalism,* Weber offered a defence of capitalism that glossed over all this blood and gore by finding spiritual origins. Capitalism, he claimed, arose as a by-product of earnest Puritan beliefs, which sought to honour God through worldly deeds. Money-making ceased to be a form of 'filthy lucre' and became a mission that provided a sign of salvation. The modern neoliberals and Max Weber shared a common approach: they sought to give capitalism a purer varnish to mask its real brutality.

Instead of an economic system founded on a 'military-industrial complex', neoliberals presented the market as an extension of democratic choice. In their utopian vision, the customer-citizen voted constantly with their credit card. The cry of the new left for freedom from oppressive structures was 'recuperated' by an ideology that offered individuality and self-development, via the market. The left critique of repressive state structures was transmuted into a right wing discourse that attacked the 'nanny state' in the name of freedom. The attacks on inequality in the economic system were countered with a shareholder populism where everyone could use their savings to play the stock markets. In brief, neoliberalism promoted a vision of market *freedom* as the essence of capitalism.

But these ideas never described how capitalism really worked. Neoliberals might sound off in the media and at university lecterns about the wonders of the market, but actual capitalists knew that the system did not work according to the textbooks. The ideologues offered general models, which accentuated pure elements, while practitioners made messy compromises, which suited their immediate economic needs. Real capitalists occasionally invoked the themes of neoliberalism – even while presiding over arrangements that contradicted them. Or, to put it differently, while neoliberalism functioned as the main ideological support for the present economic order, it did not – contrary to its own claim – actually describe existing capitalism.

Two examples illustrate the gap that existed between neoliberal ideas and the realities of capitalism.

State Spending

The core of the neoliberal discourse is a reduction in state spending. It suggests that the state should only occupy the role assigned to it by Adam Smith – that of a 'nightwatchman' who patrols the perimeter, dealing principally with public goods such as defence and policing. Accordingly, Milton Friedman held up as his ideal the level of public spending in Hong Kong, which averaged 15 per cent of GDP at the time.[24]

Contrary to the arguments of the neoliberals, however, public spending in OECD countries continued to rise until the 1990s and has only abated in some countries since then. The overall ratio of public spending to GDP stood at 41 per cent in 2003.[25] Table 2.I illustrates the pattern.

With the exception of Canada, there does not appear to be any significant drop in public spending, despite the hegemony of neo-liberalism in elite circles. This helps to explain Milton Friedman's somewhat bizarre comment in 2000 that 'the world is more social-ist today than it was in 1947'.[26]

Table 2.1: Public Spending as a Percentage of GDP in Select Countries

Year	Canada	Germany	France	UK	Japan	US
1983	48	48	52	48	32	36
1988	45	45	49	41	31	36
1993	52	49	55	46	35	38
1998	44	49	54	40	38	34
2003	40	49	54	43	38	36

Source: J. Larosiere, 'Thoughts about the European Stability and Growth Pact, Annex 1', Academie des Sciences Morales et Politique.

Market Competition

The neoliberals harked back to the days of Adam Smith where a de-regulated market led to greater competition and more choice. In reality, existing capitalism is actually dominated by ever-larger oligopolies. Ten of the largest corporations control 75 per cent of the global car industry; the six largest electrical, electronic and computer corporations control 33 per cent of their market; the six largest telecommunications corporations control 50 per cent of their market; the five largest chemical corporations control 65 per cent of their market; the seven largest pharmaceutical corpora-tions control 67 per cent of their market.[27]

Contrary to the mythology of globalisation, these corporations work closely with their respective nation states to promote their own interests. Far from functioning as rugged individuals on the marketplace, most corporations have strong political arms that they exercise via extensive lobbying. They network constantly with the political elite, and hold regular face-to-face briefings with key state officials. Corporate headquarters are normally located near the centres of political power, rather than in outlying areas where rents might be cheaper.

Moreover, as the level of concentration in each sector has increased, more economic activity takes place inside corporations rather than in the open marketplace. Huge corporations often function like planned economies. Internal bureaucracies develop to allocate resources through command structures, rather than through market mechanisms. Instead of prices being set by a market, for example, corporations use transfer pricing to artificially lower the production cost of components in some countries, and raise them in others. Far from the pure market expanding, it has in fact contracted.

Therefore, while neoliberalism motivated supporters of capitalism, it never functioned as a real economic programme to guide how the system worked. It worked only as an ideological blunderbuss to demoralise and weaken opponents.

But the agenda that gave birth to it – the transfer of wealth to the already privileged and restoring higher rates of profit – has not gone away. In the aftermath of the crash of 2008 there is, therefore, an uneasy mix between the old battle cries of the neoliberals and new demands for more state support for wealth.

SOCIALISM FOR THE RICH – NEOLIBERALISM FOR THE POOR

The new agenda of the 'post-liberals' is already clear. They want more state support for large corporations, and some regulation of the financial system. But they want to maintain the same methods of rule that were used to weaken working class organisation in the last two decades.

The strategy arises from the pattern of late capitalist development. The concentration of capital in a small number of corporations means that some bankruptcies are likely to have a devastating effect on national economies. This explains why the US President devotes so much time and money to saving gigantic auto companies like Chrysler. According to the laws of free market economics, the company should be allowed to go bankrupt so that greater profit opportunities are created for its rivals, Ford and GM. However, the danger of letting one of the 'big three' go down is that it will create a black hole, which will suck many other smaller supply firms down with it. The concern is not for the Chrysler workers, who are being forced to take wage cuts and savage new conditions. Rather, it is the effects such a collapse might have on a wider segment of US capitalism that worries the US government.

Despite a much hyped rhetoric about a borderless world, there is no 'global capitalism' today, but rather a wide range of different national nodes and networks of capital that compete in a globalised world. Political elites in nation states are embedded in dense networks which link them to the health of their largest corporations. Each state often picks out 'national champions' which they help promote in the global economy. And so each state will provide vast sums to support them in times of crisis.

Post-liberalism, therefore, means greater state intervention to prop up national capitalism. In involves the transfer of a proportion of the social surplus of society to its national corporate champions. It means forcing workers not only to accept real wage reductions but a transfer of some of their taxes to help subsidise the profits of large financial and non-financial corporations. The bigger the current bail out, the longer and greater this subsidy will be.

But while the state dispenses corporate welfare and talks tough on regulation, it still seeks to weaken worker organisation. There is no let-up in the calls for 'flexibility' and for a responsible trade unionism that knows its place. Even while the banks are being bailed out, nothing is being done to support workers who equally demand state help. When workers at Waterford

Crystal staged a seven-week-long sit-in to demand state support to protect jobs and pensions, their appeals fell on deaf ears. Similarly, workers in SR Technics received no support from the state to help maintain their jobs, even though they marched and pleaded. State intervention, it seems, is confined to supporting the wealthy.

The legacy of neoliberalism continues in many other ways. The old language about a bloated, inefficient public sector escalates, even while handouts to the private sector rise. In a rhetoric which equates the private sector with 'efficiency' and the public sector with 'waste', it is easy to forget that it was banks which managed to lose fortunes. The function of this rhetoric is to get the population to fully internalise market values. They need to understand that mysterious market forces are almost part of the natural world, of reality. When doubts start to appear, faith has to be restored with a continuous chant: private is good, public is bad. The chant will intensify because, with state intervention returning to prop up a sick system, there is a renewed danger of 'politicisation'. Some might even ask: Are we not as important as corporate leaders – unless their voices are not drowned out with the chant.

Inside the public sector itself, market mechanisms are still pushed in the post-liberal era. Thus, hospitals continue to be benchmarked against each other; league tables are created for schools; the casework of social workers is measured for 'outputs'. A vast mountain of paper work grows as artificial Key Performance Indicators are developed for every possible human activity. Wasteful exercises, with absurd titles such as Performance Management Development Systems, are administered by overpaid external consultants. The sole purpose is to convince public sector workers that they must mimic the 'real world' of the private sector, and acknowledge that their performance can be measured through fake outputs and targets. As Bourdieu put it, neoliberalism is built on a regime of artificially-induced insecurity. To support this regime, a managerialist bureaucracy expands to measure and monitor all workers below it – while adding virtually nothing to genuine public service.

Most crucially, the neoliberal focus on 'competitiveness' remains. Neoliberalism may be discredited on a global level, but its legacy for forcing every economic unit to compete directly against another remains. In some states, such as Ireland, it is taken to the level of national obsession. The whole basis of political policy has become the restoration of competitiveness. Ireland, it seems, is accelerating its race to the bottom, and means to get there before anyone else.

But does the Irish case represent only an extreme version of socialism for the rich and neoliberalism for the poor? Might not the wider changes induced by the present economic crisis become an opportunity to establish 'a form of regular and regulated capitalism' that finally dispatches neoliberalism to its grave?

A REGULAR AND REGULATED CAPITALISM?

Before the Wall Street Crash of 1929, one of the key figures in orthodox economics was John Maynard Keynes. That crash had a major impact on his ideas and, in 1936, his book *The General Theory of Employment, Interest, and Money* was published. This launched a frontal attack on the idea of self-regulating markets and the conventional notion that wage cuts were necessary to achieve a better balance between the supply and demand for labour. Keynes instead suggested that state intervention was necessary to stimulate demand in a 'counter-cyclical' way. Every dollar or pound spent, he argued, could have a 'multiplier effect' because the jobs it helped to create would lead to more spending. After the Second World War, the new orthodoxy became a 'mixed economy' where states managed the fluctuations of an unstable market.

Economists such as Paul Krugman and Joseph Stiglitz, who believe the current economic crisis offers the possibility of a return to a regular and regulated capitalism, look to Keynes as their inspiration. Keynes, however, is an ambiguous figure in many respects. Occasionally, there are strong rhetorical flourishes of radicalism, where, for example, he calls for the 'euthanasia of the rentiers' or, when writing in the *Yale Review* in 1933, he stated that:

> The decadent international but individualistic capitalism, in the hands of which we found ourselves after the [first world] war, is not a success. It is not intelligent, it is not beautiful, it is not just, it is not virtuous – and it doesn't deliver the goods. In short, we dislike it, and we are beginning to despise it. But when we wonder what to put in its place, we are extremely perplexed.[28]

But despite these occasional flashes, Keynes's aim was to save capitalism, not destroy it. Those who follow in his footsteps and advocate more regulation have a similar motivation. But they face a number of key problems in applying this to modern-day capitalism.

First, despite the depth of the crisis, most governments have concentrated on salvaging their respective financial systems, rather than intervening to create jobs. The current political agenda is exclusively dictated by capital, rather than popular pressure. There is, therefore, a form of 'Keynesianism from above' which is designed to prop up bankrupt parts of the system. In the US, President Obama has spent $787 billion on a stimulus package, but much of it consists mainly of tax breaks for business, and new opportunities for public-private partnership schemes. Far from moving in a progressive direction, the *New York Times* columnist, Paul Krugman, summed up the Obama approach thus: 'They still believe in the magic of the financial market and in the prowess of the wizards who perform the magic'.[29]

Second, while Keynes's attacks on wage-cutting deserve to be read today, the measures he advocates did not actually revive capitalism in the 1930s. The key example used to advocate a Keynesian solution is the New Deal, which was instituted by Franklin D. Roosevelt when he was inaugurated as president in 1933. He established a Civilian Construction Corp which gave work to the unemployed and introduced new regulations to control the banks. He also created a limited number of state projects, such as the Tennessee River Authority, to develop infrastructure. In his second term, Roosevelt enlisted the support of the unions and set up the Works Project Administration, which eventually employed 3.3 million people on the prevailing local wage rates. Even to this day, many US cities have parks, bridges and schools which were constructed by the WPA.

These measures gave huge relief from suffering for the unemployed, but it was not until four years after the New Deal that any sort of recovery began. Only in 1937 did the size of the US economy regain the level it achieved before 1929. But soon after this recovery, the US fell into another economic decline, which lasted until WWII. It was only the huge spending on arms and the creation of a war economy that led the way out of the last Great Depression. J.K. Galbraith summed the situation up when he wrote: 'The Great Depression of the thirties never came to an end. It merely disappeared in the great mobilisation of the forties.'[30]

This experience poses a certain problem for advocates of a regular and regulated capitalism today. If the New Deal, which had been radicalised by pressure from below, brought relief from suffering without solving the problem, might not the same thing occur today? The general systemic crisis of capitalism in the 1930s had far deeper roots than Keynes had foreseen. Even when demand was increased through state intervention, control of capital still lay in the hands of a tiny few, whose sole interest was profit. When they did not deem it profitable to invest, the economy stayed in depression, and the lives of many were shattered. If it took the deaths of over 50 million people in WWII to revive the for-profit engines of the current system, might it not be reasonable to ask: What will it take to revive the system on a sustained basis today?

Third, it is difficult to see how any effective regulation could be imposed on modern capitalism. There can certainly be a greater shift to state involvement, but this does not guarantee that capital will be controlled. One reason is that the wealthy have now acquired more than fifty years' experience of undermining state regulation. During the last depression, there were also calls for greater regulation and the Glass–Steagall Act was passed in the US in 1933 to separate commercial and investment banking. In the US, commercial banks take savings from depositors and lend them out again, whereas investment banks are free to engage in financial speculation. The effect of the act was to limit a section of the financial market from involvement in speculation. But in the 1980s, US financial corporations set out to undermine this act and, in a ten-year period, spent an estimated $5.1 billion in lobbying for its removal. Eventually, in 1999, a bill pushed through the US Houses of Congress repealed key aspects of the Glass–Steagall Act, thereby smoothing the way for the creation of financial megafirms such as Citigroup.

The US case illustrates a general pattern. The sheer size of modern corporations means they can deploy a vast array of resources to bend politicians to their will. The standard method of corruption was brown envelopes passed from a business leader to a politician to get certain favourable results. Increasingly, however, businesses prefer to rely on sophisticated forms of lobbying. Lobbyists are often recruited from former members of the political elite and have ready-made access to the networks of power.

Typically, corporations also recruit former members of the political elite to their Boards of Directors. Once again, the purpose is to network with politicians so that corporations get their way. And by recruiting insiders who have accumulated high levels of institutional knowledge, corporations can find a range of ways to achieve their aims.

The Irish political elite has been most enthusiastic in this 're-volving door' practice. Seamus Pairceir, the former chair of the Revenue Commissioners, went on to become a private consultant for Dunnes, and, at various times, a director of Salomon Brothers Funds, J.P. Morgan, Group One International Trust Managers, Legg Mason Investments and IG International Management.[31] Ray McSharry, a former Finance Minister and EU Commissioner, be-came a chairman of Eircom and a non-executive director of Bank of Ireland, and a host of other firms. Dick Spring, the former Tanaiste, became a chair of Altobridge and non-executive director of Flexco and other firms. The list could go on for some length.

Another practice used by corporations is to get their key fig-ures appointed onto commissions and advisory bodies that pro-pose changes in a law or regulatory practice. A useful example here is the current Commission on Taxation, which will produce suggestions on an overhaul of Irish tax law. It is already stuffed full of corporate representatives so that, even before it publishes a word, there is a bias. Its 17 members include three company direc-tors of financial corporations, four tax solicitors or partners in ac-countancy firms which help corporations avoid tax, the CEO of the Irish Stock Exchange, a representative of the Bankers Federa-tion, and just one token trade union official.

But all these methods pale into insignificance beside the key weapon which corporations use to undermine regulation: eco-nomic blackmail. Modern parliamentary democracy operates on a fatal separation of powers. TDs in parliament pass laws to control political structures, but unelected Boards of Directors control the economic resources on which these structures rely. Where these clash, those with money invariably call the shots. Even before these clashes begin, the parliamentarians are socialised into a mindset whereby they accept 'the realities' of corporate control and do not pass laws which upset them unduly. Corporations regularly make their views known to state officials and, in the case of Ireland, a 'frictionless' relationship is established whereby the Irish state does everything it can to serve their needs.

When any of these subtle processes break down, corporations gain leverage by calling into play less subtle forms of economic blackmail. They threaten to withdraw investment or move the location of plants to other countries which give them more favourable terms. They hide part of their vast profits in off-shore tax locations to escape any regulation. According to the General Accounting Office in the US, for example, more than 60 per cent of US corporations with at least $250 million in assets (representing 93 per cent of all corporate assets) reported no federal tax liability each year between 1996 and 2000.[32] The main reason is that they were using tax havens. If corporations can hide away such vast amounts of profit, the chances of developing a regular and regulated capitalism are zero. Globalisation has given extra leverage to corporations and they will use it to bend any government to their will.

Instead of seeking a regular and regulated capitalism, therefore, we need to question the very fundamentals of the system and look at ways of establishing a 'not-for-profit economy'. That entails returning to the ideas of the greatest critic of the system, Karl Marx, to see why the system is fundamentally flawed, and why we need to urgently push for change.

Endnotes

[1] International Labour Organisation, *Global Employment Trends* (ILO: Geneva, 2009).

[2] 'Job Losses Pose a threat to stability world wide', *New York Times*, 15 February 2009.

[3] 'Violent unrest rocks China as crisis hits', *Sunday Times* 1 February 2009.

[4] C. Loser, *Major Contagion and Shocking loss of Wealth* (Asian Development Bank, 2009) p. 19.

[5] M. Whitney, *Financial Meltdown: Haircut Time for Bondholders*, Global Research, 12 March 2009.

[6] 'Shipping rates hit zero as trade sinks', *Daily Telegraph*, 14 January 2009.

[7] A. de Tocqueville, *The Old Regime and the Revolution* (Chicago: University of Chicago Press, 2004), p. 222.

[8] 'Mr Risk Goes to Washington', *Business Week*, 12 June 2006.

[9] T. Friedman, *The Lexus and the Olive Tree* (London: Harper Collins, 2006) p. 106.

[10] M. Friedman, *Capitalism and Freedom* (Chicago: University of Chicago Press, 1982), p. vi.

[11] A. Ebenstein, *Hayek's Journey: The Mind of Frederich Hayek* (Basingstoke: Palgrave, 2003), p. 96.

[12] F. Hayek, *Law, Legislation and Liberty: Vol. 1, Rules and Order* (London: Routledge and Kegan Paul, 1973), p. 2.

[13] N. Bosanquet, *After the New Right* (Aldershot, Heinemann, 1984), p. 39.

[14] E. Fama, 'Efficient Capital Markets: A Review of Theory and Empirical Work, *Journal of Finance, American Finance Association*, vol. 25(2), 1970, pp. 383-417, May.

[15] L. Lapham, 'Tentacles of Rage', *Harpers Magazine* 1 September 2004, p. 4.

[16] J. Gelinas, *Juggernaut Politics: Understanding Predatory Globalization* (London: Zed, 2003), p. 120.

[17] J. Stiglitz, *Globalisation and its Discontent* (London: Penguin, 2002), p. 41.

[18] See G. Stigler, 'Director's Law of Public Income Redistribution', *Journal of Law and Economics*, Vol.13, No. 1, 1970.

[19] P. Bourdieu, *Political Interventions* (London: Verso, 2008), p. 288.

[20] U. Beck, *Brave New World at Work* (Cambridge: Polity Press, 2000), p. 89.

[21] Testimony of Alan Greenspan to Committee on Government Oversight and Reform, 23 October 2008.

[22] Speech by Alan Greenspan on World Finance and Risk Management, Lancaster House, 25 September 2002.

[23] FSA Press Release, 18 March 2009.

[24] M. Friedman, 'The Hong Kong Experiment', *The Hoover Digest*, 1998 No 3.

[25] I. Journard, P. Kongsrud, Y. Narn, R. Price, 'Enhancing the Effectiveness of Public Spending: Experience in OECD Countries', *OECD Economic Studies*, No 37, 2003, pp. 110-160.

[26] Commanding Heights: Interview with Milton Friedman on Public Broadcasting Service 10 January 2000 www.pbs.org/wgbh/ commandingheights/shared.minitext/int_miltonfriedman.html

[27] Figures from Fortune Global 500 and Financial Times Top 500.

[28] J. Maynard Keynes, 'National Self Sufficiency', *Yale Review*, Vol. 22, No. 4 (June 1933) pp. 755 -769.

[29] P. Krugman, 'Market Mystique', *New York Times*, 26 March 2009.

[30] J.K. Galbraith, *American Capitalism* (New Brunswick: Transaction, 1993) p. 65.

[31] 'How Tax Chief's Retirement was Haunted by a Number of Lurid Headlines', *Irish Independent*, 21 December 2006.

[32] GAO, *Tax Administration: Comparison of the Reported tax liabilities of Foreign and US controlled corporations 1996-2000*. (Washington: GAO, 2004).

3

CAPITALISM IS NOT WORKING

THE MOST COMMON EXPLANATION for the current economic crisis is that it has been caused by 'speculators' who created a 'casino economy'. The story goes that banks, property developers and, behind them, a set of hedge funds and other financial wizards, stoked up a huge bubble that has now crashed. One merit of this explanation is that it cuts through the excuses offered by conventional economists who talk in abstract categories. Typically, they refer to 'imbalances' between savings and consumption without ever mentioning which social class gained or lost. But there are two important weaknesses in the explanation about speculation.

First, it is no longer possible to draw a neat dividing line between financial speculators and the wider capitalist class. The division between finance capital and industrial capital broke down a long time ago and now all corporations engage in 'financial engineering'. A corporation such as General Motors sells cars but it also has its own financial wing, General Motors Acceptance Corporation, which became a bank in its own right and made profits of $2.4 billion in 2004. Its sale raised $14 billion for GM. Similarly, General Electric is no longer solely a manufacturing firm because half its revenues come from its various financial wings. Indeed, many commentators now see it as a financial corporation with manufacturing wings. The integration of financial and industrial capital is also evident in the interlocking directorships of the fi-

nancial and non-financial companies. The board of the ill-famed
Lehman Brothers, for example, included the former chair of IBM,
the former head of Halliburton, the former head of the media
group Telemundo (who is also a director of Sony and MGM) and
the current chair of GlaxoSmithKline (who is also a former head
of Vodafone). The board of the investment bank, Goldman Sachs,
includes directors of General Motors, Mobil Oil, Novartis, Kraft
Foods, Colgate Palmolive, Du Pont, Texas Instrument, Boeing and
ArcelorMittal.[1]

The second problem with simply blaming speculators is that it
ignores the problems that were building up in capitalism before
the current crash. Economic historian Robert Brenner has described the period since the 1970s as the 'long downturn'.[2] Before
this period, capitalism had had a 'Golden Age' in which growth
rates were consistently high, and during which time the boom
and slump cycle receded.

Since the 1970s, however, there has been a pattern of huge dis-
locations which have brought suffering on a vast scale. Profit rates
have dipped and unemployment has veered upwards. And countries that were once economic success stories have experienced
crashes from which they have had difficulty recovering. The most
dramatic example is Japan, which was once regarded as the
world's second economic superpower. But Japan's capitalist
economy has stagnated now for a decade and a half. Countries in
East Asia experienced an influx of foreign capital in the 1990s but
were then devastated by a crash in 1997. In Indonesia, for example, the currency lost 80 per cent of its value overnight, and its
GDP shrank by 15 per cent.[3] Other countries in Eastern Europe
that underwent the 'shock therapy' of privatisation to reap the
rewards of the 'free market' have also been devastated.

The current crisis is unique because it has hit the very core of
the global system and has led to a global contraction. Even within
the core zone of industrialised countries, problems have been apparent for some time. As economic performance has declined, the

system has needed periodic bubbles to add vitality and growth. From the 1990s onwards, these bubbles played an increasingly important and disruptive role. There was a stock market bubble and then a 'dot com' bubble when absurd prices were paid for internet firms. After that blew, there was a telecommunications bubble when vast sums rushed into fibre optic cables. After it broke, the *Economist* claimed that 'the telecoms bust is some ten times bigger than the better known dotcom crash: the rise and fall of telecoms may indeed qualify as the largest bubble in history'.[4] The prophecy was mistaken because the property bubble was even bigger. And even when that burst, there was a brief surge of speculation on food prices.

The last global economic *upturn* before the present crash was the weakest ever in the post-war period. Growth was lower, fewer extra workers were employed and there was a huge glut in savings as capitalists failed to re-invest their profits back into industry. According to one report from JP Morgan Securities:

> The real driver of this saving glut has been the corporate sector. Between 2000 and 2004, the switch from corporate dis-savings to net savings across the G6, (France, Germany, US, Japan, Britain and Italy) economies amounted to over €1 trillion.... The rise in corporate savings has thus been truly global spanning three regions – North America, Europe and Japan.[5]

Something was going radically wrong – and most of the normal economic commentators did not understand why. There were some attempts to blame Alan Greenspan, Chair of the US Federal Reserve, for creating a bubble through loose credit policies. But this ignores the more fundamental question: why had modern capitalism entered a long downturn where growth became more dependent on bubbles, and where there was a reluctance among capitalists to invest in production?

Answering that question requires a return to Marx.

THE GHOST OF MARX

Marx was not a conventional economist. He sought to demystify the workings of the economy in order to unmask conflicts between employers and workers over the distribution of the world's resources. His great work, *Capital*, is a clear theoretical study and is renowned for its insight. But *Capital* also reverberates with anger against injustice.

He wrote, for example, that 'capital is dead labour, which, vampire-like, lives by sucking living labour, and lives the more, the more labour it sucks'.[6] He mocked those who justified the employment of child labour as necessary for efficiency and competitiveness. He suggested that 'children were quietly slaughtered for the sake of their delicate fingers, just as horned cattle are slaughtered in Southern Russia for their hide and fat'.[7] He described how early capitalism came into existence, 'dripping from head to toe, from every pore, with dirt and blood'.[8]

Of course, conventional social scientists dislike this sort of outrage, and argue that one has to be 'value free', to be an objective 'scientist'. But their claim of objectivity, through adopting a 'neutral' position, is often dishonest. Under the guise of simply describing 'realities', they often function as advocates for wealthy and powerful groups, sometimes consciously, whilst at other times unconsciously. Economists who claim to be describing market forces in order to read off detailed policy measures are hardly neutral. The hollowness of their rhetoric is revealed when we ask: Why do they never advocate an increase in wages or a reduction in profits? Why do they never claim that an increase in social welfare might be good for society? If they were genuinely neutral in a conflict between social classes, they could hardly *always* ask workers to 'restrain' their wages, and never mention profits.

Marx was able to be both objective and passionate because he saw capitalism as a social relationship. It was not a thing or a system that existed independently of human beings, but a real living relationship between different classes of people. He objected to a reified form of thinking, where categories such as 'market forces' appear as natural or even quasi-spiritual forces to which we have to submit. This, he argued, was like a fetishistic form of religion. 'Fetishism', contrary to its modern sexual overtones, originally came from the Portuguese word *feiticio,* and was used by early merchants to describe a religious practice which venerated objects, thought to be animated by spirits. More broadly, fetishism refers to a practice whereby objects, which are created by human beings, come to dominate them. They are thought to exist independently of people's will and so are considered worthy of adoration. In brief, this is a description which aptly summarises the mindset of a conventional economist when analysing 'market forces'.

Marx liberated himself from any such thinking by asserting that capitalism is based on a relationship between two different kinds of commodity owners:

> ... on the one hand, the owners of money, means of production, means of subsistence, who are eager to increase the sum of values they possess, by buying other people's labour-power;

> ... on the other hand, free labourers, the sellers of their own labour-power, and, therefore, the sellers of labour.

> Free labourers, in the double sense that neither they themselves form part and parcel of the means of production, as in the case of slaves, bondsmen, etc., nor do the means of production belong to them, as in the case of peasant-proprietors;

> ... they are, therefore, free from, unencumbered by, any means of production of their own.[9]

The key issue is what occurs when 'free labourers' – or modern employees – sell their labour to the owner of the means of production. For conventional economists, this is simply another market transaction: a worker sells their labour and the employer buys that labour at prices guided by the laws of supply and demand. On the surface then, a fair and equal exchange – except that our modern economist would never use such a morally loaded term as 'fair'.

Marx opposes this argument on two grounds. First, the 'object' at the core of this transaction – human labour – is not a commodity like any other. It is not a lump of coal, a computer part or a litre of petrol, and cannot simply be treated as such. It is the life energy of the worker, intimately connected with their very being as a human. Its sale and purchase, therefore, raises questions about freedom and human capacity.

Secondly, behind the appearance of equality lies a fundamental *inequality*. For what the worker sells is not a definite quantity of 'labour' in exchange for a set wage, but, rather, an indefinite 'labour power' in exchange for a definite wage. The worker is not allowed to bargain whether or not they can give a 60 per cent commitment in exchange for a €500 a week wage, or an 80 per cent commitment for a €600 week wage. This very question appears absurd because the buyer of labour power has the full freedom to consume their commodity in any way they see fit. That, after all, is also the rule of the 'free' market.

There is, therefore, a sharp contradiction between the rhetoric about market 'freedom' and the reality of tyranny in the sphere of production. In the sphere of circulation, Marx writes sarcastically that there is 'a very Eden of the innate rights of Man. It is the exclusive realm of Freedom, Equality, Property and Bentham'.[10] Freedom because buyers and sellers transact their commodity by their own free will; Equality because they appear to exchange equivalent commodities; Property because each disposes of what they own; Bentham, because according to the nineteenth century utilitarian philosopher, each looks only to his own advantage.

But once we leave the marketplace and cross the threshold marked 'No Admittance Except on Business', tyranny prevails. By tyranny in this context, we do not mean brutality or terror – although this can and does still occur, especially on some production lines around the world. We simply mean that, once labour power has been bought, it is totally under the control of the employer. The employer has the full freedom to use the labour *power* they purchased in whatever way will yield the most return. They will, therefore, use this purchase to produce more value than the wages advanced for its purchase.

This gives rise to Marx's distinction between *necessary labour time*, when the worker is producing the equivalent in value to that which he or she will receive in a wage, and *surplus labour*, when he or she is working for free for the employer. The difference between surplus and necessary labour time points to the rate of exploitation that a worker experiences. It also lays the basis for the profit, or what Marx called surplus value.

This brief detour is necessary to understand Marx's argument about why capitalism is an inherently unstable system. For his central purpose was not to simply describe the system but to unearth its contradictions. If capitalism could simply maintain the profit system through this relatively smooth process of exploitation we have just described, it would not experience periodic crisis.

But there is a contradiction between the ability of the employer to exploit labour in the sphere of production, and their capacity to realise profits by selling in the market place. This contradiction arises from the fact that, although the modern economy makes people more dependent on each other than at any time in history, it is controlled by a tiny number of people whose sole goal is profit.

The division of labour required to produce the smallest commodity has no parallel in human history. In order to acquire a
simple cup of coffee, for example, a purchaser will depend on the
labour of Ethiopian peasants and dockers, administrative staff in
New York trading houses, shipping agents, warehouse staff and,
finally, restaurant staff. This complex social division of labour is
directed by a tiny number of people who make decisions without
being aware of key decisions made by others.

Having purchased labour power, each individual employer
seeks to use it as 'efficiently as possible', and then increase market
share to realise profits. Inside their own workplace, they relent-
lessly seek to reduce unit costs, in order to increase 'competitiveness', by all manner of methods. They seek to intensify work while
keeping wages down; they cut holiday pay, shift premiums, pension entitlements; they try to hire new staff on rates that are lower
than existing staff. And the more they succeed, the more they will
increase the level of surplus labour time.

But it is not an option to do this while maintaining a static
level of production, because competition between capitalists
forces each to produce ever more goods, and to re-invest a large
proportion of their profits back into production.

Strangely enough, the best capitalists are not those who per-
sonally consume profits to fund a luxury lifestyle – although
many do – but those who are driven by the bug: 'accumulate for
accumulation's sake'. In other words, simply produce to make
profit to make more profit.

But whilst this behaviour is rational for each individual capitalist, it produces periodic problems for the wider system. In particular, it leads to the problem of over-production, because, as
Marx put it:

> Since the aim of capital is not to minister to certain
> wants, but to produce profit, a rift must continually en-
> sue between the limited dimensions of consumption un-

der capitalism and a production which forever tends to exceed this immanent barrier. Furthermore, capital consists of commodities, and therefore over-production of capital implies over-production of commodities.[11]

Overproduction does not mean that there are too many goods and services that people do not need. Rather, the mass of people may be short of goods or services, but cannot afford to buy them because they have been driven out of work or because their wages are too low. This can occur in a number of ways.

First, the lack of co-ordination in the market means that there is a ceaseless drive to produce more products for which there is a profit, regardless of the decisions of other producers. The absence of planning means that no prior provision is made for the supply of raw materials, or for training labour up to the required standards. As a result, inflation can rise rapidly under boom conditions and can catch individual corporations on the hop, forcing them to cut back. But this, in turn, can have a trigger effect, which impacts on others down the supply chain. The market depends on the spending of others – either the spending of fellow capitalists on luxury items, plant and equipment, or on the spending of workers in shops. Breaking the chain at decisive points chokes off a boom, and turns it into a recession.

Second, the attempt by every corporation to reduce wage costs while producing ever more goods comes into conflict with each other. If the wages are held down by competitive pressures, then workers eventually have less money to buy the collective goods that are produced. This also leads to overproduction – because workers cannot buy the goods that have been produced. These goods may, of course, be desperately needed by human beings – but if they cannot be bought, there is no market. They pile up in warehouses while employers complain about 'excess capacity'. Sometimes, this problem can be overcome if capitalists themselves stimulate the economy by greater investment in capital goods – in machinery, factory space and office space – which creates more jobs and wage packets.

But the system runs into another problem here. Capitalism suffers from a longer-term tendency for the rate of profit to fall. Marx's argument was a little more complex on this score. But, essentially, this tendency arose from the fact that the 'organic composition' of capital changes over a period. This means that the ratio between the levels of capital investment to the amount of labour employed shifts dramatically in favour of the former.

The first capitalist who tools up with new machinery and employs fewer workers will normally make greater profits. They gain a 'first mover advantage' because they sell their goods at relatively high prices but use new machinery, which cheapens the cost of production. But other capitalists eventually follow suit. Soon, capital investment rises, but the price of goods falls because it takes less labour to produce them. Capitalists must now try to get higher levels of profit from an ever smaller number of workers. But the rate of surplus value they extract compared to the amount of investment they have employed will tend to decline.

Faced with this tendency for the rate of profit to fall, capitalists can try to invoke a number of countervailing measures. They can try to increase the *absolute* level of surplus value by ensuring that a smaller number of workers work longer hours. They can do this by a range of methods: they can eliminate overtime payments or shift premiums which compensate workers for unsocial hours. Or they can shift production to countries where longer hours are legal.

More commonly, they can try to increase *relative* surplus value by getting workers to produce goods that are equivalent to their own wages in a shorter part of the working day. Instead of producing goods to the value of their own wages in four hours, they do so in three or two. In this way, more of the working day is devoted to working for free for their employer. This can be achieved through intensifying work effort. If we imagine the working day as a piece of Swiss cheese, where there are several holes called 'down time', the employer will try to fill in as many as possible. Under the cry of 'flexibility', they will seek to achieve a high continuous work effort or, to put it differently, to attain extra productivity while paying the same wages.

Finally, employers can also seek to reduce wages in order to restore profit levels. They can do this by imposing wage cuts; by employing younger workers on lower wage rates than older counterparts; by paying wage rises that are less than the rate of inflation; or they can close down and rehire workers on lower wage rates or they can move production to areas where labour is paid less.

All of these methods appear in modern society and sometimes they partially restore profitability. But the more they succeed, the more they reduce the buying power of workers and feed into the problem of over-production. And when profit rates are only partially restored, this can also lead to reluctance by capitalists to invest in new plant and equipment. The slowing of investment then leads to 'excess savings' and this, too, feeds into the wider problem of reduced markets for others.

One way out of this conundrum is an economic crisis itself. When millions are sacked, and plant and equipment are mothballed, the surviving capitalists can buy these up at much cheaper rates. They can eliminate their rivals and gain extra market share, while cheapening the cost of investment and hiring labour. In this process, which the Austrian economist Joseph Schumpeter called 'creative destruction', the lives of real human beings – not just abstract commodities – are destroyed through poverty and unemployment. But this is how the system increasingly breathes – by stumbling from one economic disaster to another.

WALL STREET CRASH 2008

How do these general theories – developed over 150 year ago – help us understand what is happening today? There have been many changes in the world since Marx was writing, with state intervention in economies, for example, being much higher. At the time Marx wrote *Capital*, state spending only represented 10 per cent of GDP[12] but it is normally four times higher today. Nevertheless, there is considerable evidence to indicate that the central concepts he used to understand the dynamic of the system still apply.

Marx is particularly relevant when we try to understand what occurred in global capitalism after the ending of its Golden Age in the early 1970s. There is broad evidence, for example, that the rate of profit in manufacturing in the major industrial economies declined at the start of this period. Writers such as Brenner, Dumeneil and Levy, Mosley and Harman have all charted this decline using empirical data.[13] Figure 3.1 illustrates a long period of decline which accelerates from the late 1960s.

Figure 3.1: US, German and Japanese Manufacturing Net Profits Rates[26]

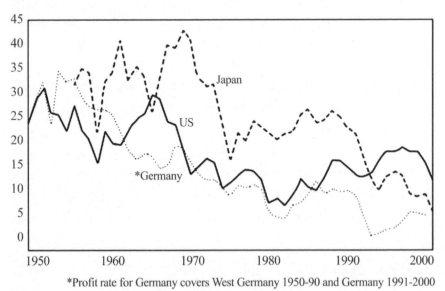

*Profit rate for Germany covers West Germany 1950-90 and Germany 1991-2000

Source: *The Economics of Global Turbulence* (London: Verso 2006) p. 7

From the early 1980s, a determined effort was made to increase profitability and a number of mechanisms were used to weaken organised labour. At a political level, a full frontal offensive was launched, symbolised by Reagan firing air traffic controllers who were members of the PATCO union in 1981 and Thatcher's later defeat of the miners. At the macroeconomic level, there was the Volker deflation of 1980-82 in the US and similar measures in Britain, when unemployment was allowed to rise so as to weaken the labour unions. At the level of the individual firm, there was a rise in corporate raiders led by the junk bond king, Michael Milken, which imposed huge debts on the firms they took over and then rapidly divested them of units whose rate of return was not high enough to satisfy the financiers.

Employers also resorted to globalisation – to move some production to developing countries and to use the threat of *further* relocations to reduce wage costs. In the G8 countries plus Australia and the Netherlands, the share of imported manufacturing inputs increased from 6 per cent in 1980 to 10 per cent in 2003.[14] The shift in production abroad was not as dramatic as some predicted but the 'whipsawing' effect was significant.

This employer offensive opened a gap between productivity and wages. Up to the end of the 1960s, it was assumed that workers had a right to a fair share of the national cake. If the cake expanded through increased productivity, workers were entitled to an extra slice. If they worked harder, their employer got the bigger portion of increased sales but workers still got a share. This began to change, however, with the new offensive. The change was most dramatic in the US, where productivity kept rising even as wage levels flat lined, as Figure 3.2 illustrates. Since 1973, total productivity growth has risen by 83 per cent, meaning that workers produce far more goods and services in a given hour of work. Yet the overall compensation package for US workers rose by only 9 per cent.[15] The situation of manual and routine clerical workers was even worse. Real average weekly earnings of private

production and non-supervisory workers actually fell by 6.5 per
cent from €581 a week to €543.65, while the hours worked per
year grew from 1,679 a year to 1.864 a year.[16] Despite much dis-
cussion of the polarisation of the workforce by educational quali-
fication, both college-educated as well as non-college-educated
workers experienced the productivity wage-gap since the mid-
1990s.

*Figure 3.2: Index of Productivity and Hourly Compensation of
Production and Non-supervisory Workers in USA (1961–2005)*

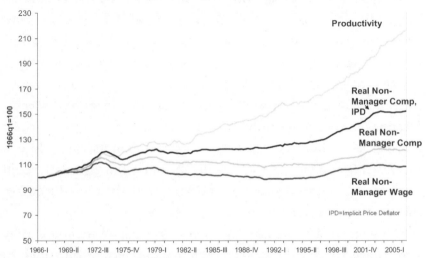

Source: J. Bernstein and L. Mishel, 'The Growing Gap between Productivity and
Earnings', http//www.national-economists.org/news/bernstein_paper.pdf.

This gap between the productivity of workers and their earnings, which Marx predicted as a response to the falling rate of
profit, has been generalised throughout the world. One sign of its
effects is a decline in labour's share of the wealth of national
economies. An IMF report on globalisation noted that labour's
share of GDP in Europe and Japan has fallen by 10 per cent since
1980, with the highest falls occurring in Ireland, Austria and the
Netherlands.[17]

This pattern of intensified exploitation of workers was designed to increase profits. And profit rates did, in fact, recover in industrialised countries from 1982 onwards but, crucially, they only made up half the decline on the previous period. A record wave of bankruptcies in the recession of 1980-81 created new opportunities for surviving corporations to buy up plant and equipment and take greater market share. Within industry, the defeats imposed on workers produced a greater proportion of surplus value relative to the wages paid. But relative to the capital invested, it did not bring back the rates of profit that had existed in the 1960s.

In the US, the rate of profit rebounded by 3.6 per cent between 1979 and 1997, after it had fallen by 5.4 per cent from 1966-1979.[18] Fred Moseley calculated that it recovered about 40 per cent of its earlier decline.[19] Dumeneil and Levy argue that the profit rate in 1997 was still only between 60 and 75 per cent of its average value for the decade 1956–65.[20]

The partial recovery in the rate of profit meant that the system faced two problems. First, by driving down the share of economies devoted to workers, it ran into the difficulty as workers could not buy all the goods produced. But, second, because the recovery in the rate of profit was only partial, there was a lower incentive to invest in productive activity. This weakness in turn meant that capitalists did not make up for the slack caused by workers' declining purchasing power.

These problems help explain why the level of investment by capitalists in advanced economies was quite sluggish. After profit rates recovered in the 1980s, there was an increase in investment rates in the 1990s, but these were not sustained. The last upturn of the twenty-first century was, in fact, based on spectacularly low levels of investment. Gross fixed capital formation fell dramatically in advanced countries in the period 2000–2009 when compared with the equivalent period in the 1990s, from an average of 3.4 per cent per year to 1.8 per cent per year.[21] This means that this last boom was the weakest ever on record.

But this was part of a wider pattern that had emerged during the 1990s – capitalists were simply not investing in productive plant with any great enthusiasm. If we examine the wider pattern of US capitalism in the twentieth century, we find that nine out of the ten years which had the lowest net non-residential fixed investment as a per cent of GDP were in the 1990s and 2000s (see Figure 3.3). Between 1986 and 2006, in only one year, 2000 – just before the stock market crash – did the per cent of GDP, represented by net private non-residential fixed investment, reach the average for 1960–79.[22]

Figure 3.3: Net Private Non-residential Fixed Investment as a Percentage of GDP (five-year moving average)

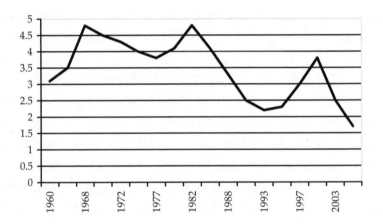

Source: Bureau of Economic Analysis, National Income and Product Accounts, Table 5.2.5. Gross and Net Domestic Investment by Major Type, Annual Data 1929-2006; Economic Report of the President, 2008, Table B-1. Gross Domestic Product, 1959-2007.

The overall pattern in advanced economies, therefore, was one of a declining labour share and sluggish patterns of investment, where growth rates were much less than in the Golden Age. The system was getting older and was showing lower signs of energy. It needed to be regularly stimulated by a series of bubbles. During this period, however, a new model emerged that appeared to produce success. It was not designed consciously but was stumbled on by accident rather than design. It was a model built on debt and speculation. It has three main elements: surplus from Chinese workers, debt-induced spending from workers in the advanced industrialised countries, and an orgy of speculation.

THE CHINA SYNDROME

One of the most remarkable economic developments of the twentieth century has been the transformation of China into the second most powerful economy. Its economy grew at a spectacular rate of around 8 per cent a year in the 1990s and in the early twenty-first century. It was powered by an industrial revolution that turned it into one of the key manufacturing centres of the world.

China presents a panoramic vision of Marx's description of capitalism because the exploitation of workers is intense: the average monthly wage is less than $80. This is just 5 per cent of wages in the US. With the turn to privatisation after 1992, Chinese workers were shaken out of the traditional 'iron rice bowl' which guaranteed them job security, medical care, child care, pensions and subsidised housing in return for low wages. Hundreds of millions had to move out of the countryside to find work in the cities and work under sweatshop conditions. According to a Chinese government survey, half of these urban residents and 90 per cent of rural residents have no medical insurance. Among those who died from diseases in some poor provinces, some 60 to 80 per cent would have survived had they been able to afford medical treatments.[23]

Such intense levels of exploitation created a Valhalla for multinational corporations and many rushed to open factories in China. As a result, Chinese exports tripled in value from $121 billion in 1994 to $365 billion in 2003. But, according to Morgan Stanley's chief economist, Stephan Roach, 65 per cent of this was 'traceable to outsourcing by Chinese subsidiaries of multinational corporations and joint ventures.'[24] By 2004, foreign firms were responsible for 54 per cent of China's exports.[25] Naturally, the sole goal of production was profit and capital accumulation, rather than human need. Instead of increasing the wages of Chinese workers, and allowing them to buy some of the vast quantities of goods produced, every effort was made to repress and create a highly flexible 'informal workforce'.[26] This led to a huge accumulation of capital even in comparison to China's large workforce.

Where was all this surplus to go? If capital accumulation had continued in a closed economic circuit, the boom would have turned to bust, as Marx classically suggested. Chinese capitalism would have faced the problem of over-production as a result of its intense exploitation of workers. However, a novel solution had also emerged: to take 'excess savings' from China and deposit them in the US.

The *Financial Times* journalist Martin Wolf has written an interesting book which examines this export of capital from China and its role in the global system. Although he can never quite acknowledge a conflict between social classes, there is more than a hint of it in this explanation:

> The Chinese government told state enterprises to become profitable and they have done what they were told. The corporate sector has become profitable by disposing of surplus workers, yet the government has not taken some increased profits as dividends on the assets it owns, even to finance a safety net for displaced workers. Remarkably (and shockingly) the government has left the money with the enterprise insiders. But the government is also a large saver. China has about 800 million poor people, yet the country now consumes less than half of GDP and exports capital to the rest of the world. This is peculiar.[27]

Chinese workers produce so much and receive so little in return, that much of its impoverished population has to share out only half of what the country produces. Vast amounts of the surplus are held in foreign currency reserves, principally in the US. Peculiar indeed, if there was not a peculiar logic to capitalism. And despite the fact that the regime sometimes claims it is 'communist', this is precisely what China is.

This unusual and temporary solution arose partially as a result of the experience of East Asian governments after the 1997 crash when the IMF won control over their economies. Guided by its neoliberal dogmas, the IMF pushed through measures of 'liberalisation', which made their predicament worse. After this experience, governments in many developing countries vowed never again to fall into the clutches of the IMF by quickly paying off their loans to the agency, and cutting their ties to it. To safeguard themselves against the withdrawal of foreign capital, they built up huge foreign reserves, which were invested in the US. The dollar was the world's reserve currency and deposits there were seen as secure. From the start of 2002 to 2007, foreign governments invested €1.64 trillion in the US, the vast majority of it in government securities.

China and the oil-producing countries led the way. China's transfers are often referred to as 'excess savings'. But they were only excess within the logic of capitalism because, if deployed in China, they threatened even greater economic dislocation. To put it more precisely, then, the Chinese elite and their multinational friends transferred the profits made from super exploitation of Chinese workers because they *needed* to keep wages low to stay ahead of rivals in the global market.

They had an additional reason for so doing. Having turned their country towards an export strategy, they did not want to bring about a revaluation of their currency, the Yuan, and a corresponding devaluation of the dollar. By keeping a huge amount of Chinese state savings in the US, they kept the dollar high, maintained favourable export markets, and avoided what happened to Japan after the Plaza Accord of 1985, when they were forced to revalue the Japanese Yen, and thus cede ground in export markets to the US.

Despite its weakening role in the global economy, the US benefited considerably from this flow of resources. It used them to become the 'global lender and purchaser of last resort'. About 70 per cent of the surplus savings of the rest of the world flowed into the US, and allowed it to fund a current account deficit of about 7 per cent of its GDP. This was worth around €2 billion per day, and, as Martin Wolf put it, 'this was the equivalent of not just a free lunch but an apparently ongoing free banquet'.[28] It also allowed the US empire to maintain its military capacity and ensure that the dollar remained the principal currency of the world. As the dollar was not tied to any fixed standard, the US could increase its paper supply, and so underpin enormous levels of debt.

A strange symbiotic relationship, therefore, developed between the elites of the world's two great rival powers. The Chinese government kept wages down in their own country, and recycled vast sums into dollars, to keep the price of their exports down. The US gained access to cheap credit, which it used to stimulate a series of economic bubbles which lifted the world economy. So stable did this arrangement appear that it has been named Bretton Woods Two. The first Bretton Woods agreement of 1947 established the dollar as the global reserve currency, and produced a stable financial order until it broke down in 1971. Optimistic commentators thought that Bretton Woods Two would bring a similar stability because it was based on the 'free choice' of China to lend to the US. And with this benign arrangement, it was thought, high levels of consumption by US households would allow the global economy to continue its upward ascent.

DEBT-INDUCED GROWTH

The influx of savings from the rest of the world allowed the US to cut interest rates in a spectacular fashion and cheapen the cost of borrowing. After the stock market crash of 2000, interest rates dropped from 6.5 per cent to 3.5 per cent in a few months. Then after 11 September 2001, when fears of an economic crash increased, they were cut further until they reached 1 per cent in 2003. This opened the way for an explosion of debt and that in turn provided a temporary solution to Marx's problem of overproduction.

One of the key targets for lending was low and middle income households. In the past, certain barriers existed to borrowings by working people and credit was often confined to better off groups. Typically, they had to approach a paternalistic bank manager who asked detailed questions to establish if they were creditworthy. Borrowings were limited through a definite link between repayments and a proportion of a normal wage. Rarely were workers allowed to take out a mortgage if repayments amounted to more than 80 per cent of their salary for 20 years. This model was shattered in recent years and cheap credit became available for all.

Cheap, mass credit became the stimulus for a property bubble that has been stoked up in many countries. According to the *Economist*, the world housing bubble between 2000 and 2005 was the biggest of all time, outrunning even that of 1929.[29] The US, Britain, Ireland, Australia and Spain were particularly affected by the mania. Banks, which in the past discarded the working class market, shifted with unseemly haste to dish out loans. If incomes were low, there was no problem taking out a 40- rather than a 20-year mortgage. To speed matters up, online forms could be filled in, and, unless you breached some really blatant red line criteria, the loan was yours.

In the US, the total value of home mortgages tripled between 1998 and 2006. American consumers also cashed in about 10 per cent of the apparent values of their homes to borrow for cars, home improvements, and credit card debts. This debt-induced growth fuelled a consumer boom which sucked in goods from other economies around the world. When the banks ran out of 'prime' credit worthy workers, they found innovative ways to increase the market. The 'sub-prime market' expanded credit lines to the poor as the banks thought they could always seize back their houses at no loss to themselves because the houses would continue to rise in value. The sub-prime market increased from 7 per cent of all US mortgages in 2000 to 20 per cent in 2006. The most extreme cases were the NINJA –'No Income, No Job, and No Assets – loans.

Debt, then, was like an elastic band that was stretched to cover the decline in real wages. It helped to overcome one aspect of the over-production problem that Marx had envisaged. If workers could not buy the vast quantities of commodities that were produced, they could at least borrow to fund their purchases. By 2005, Merrill Lynch estimated that half of all US growth came from housing-related purchases, including furniture, fittings and refurbishment. Half of all private sector jobs created since 2001 were also in this sector. The extension of working class debt expanded the market, but it also, of course, brought a huge hangover. In the US, the average person spends 14 per cent of their income just on servicing their debts.[30]

Looked at from this vantage point, Ireland is a microcosm of the US model, with one difference: Cheap credit flowed in from the savings of German pensioners to the Irish banking system, rather than from the foreign reserves of developing countries. But once it became available, the credit was used by banks to promote a similar model of growth. In Ireland, the ratio of personal debt to disposable income has also increased from 48 per cent in 1995 to 113 per cent in 2004. The expected rise in houses prices also allowed people to borrow more – even though the whole structure was built on a bubble. Between 2001 and 2007, household assets had increased by 90 per cent, mainly due to rising house prices, and so this led many people to borrow more. Consequently, debt grew by 214 per cent.[31] The collapse of house prices in both the US and Ireland, therefore, leaves many in a precarious position.

But debt was not confined to personal household debt. *Corporate* debt has also expanded dramatically, for both financial and non-financial corporations. Business debt exploded in the US between 1997 and 2005, growing from 66 per cent to over 100 per cent of its GDP.[32] Financial corporations led the way by increasing their debt from 10 per cent of overall debt in the 1970s, to one-third in more recent times.[33] Bankers were once just lenders but they then became major borrowers on inter-bank markets.

Why, then, was everyone so keen to borrow and fall into debt if this period of capitalism was characterised by excess savings due to a reluctance by capitalists to invest in productive activity? To understand the answer, we need to examine the third element of the model which allowed global capitalism to temporarily overcome some of its intrinsic problems.

THE SPECULATIVE JUNGLE

As we have seen, many capitalists became unsure about re-investing in industry and services because of the problem of over-production and declining rates of profits. Their 'excess savings' found their way instead into speculative activities. The more corporations turned to speculation to use up their 'excess savings', the more they also borrowed to gain more 'leverage' to join in the orgy of speculation. If you find, for example, that you can get a 30 per cent rate of return on speculation, rather than 7 or 8 per cent through investing in industry, you will borrow more to take out a bigger bet. You will assume that your debts will be paid off so fast that you can enter a new round of speculative activities. It is, of course, driven by greed – but capitalism is based on organised greed.

The opportunities for speculation increased enormously in recent decades. One stimulus, for example, was the growth of household debt itself. Higher levels of household debt encouraged banks and finance houses to develop 'financial instruments' which used supposedly clever techniques to 'spread risk', and make money from spreading that risk. In the US, commercial banks became 'originators' who dispensed mortgages, and then sold on the rights to collect interest to investment banks. These pooled together a host of mortgages by 'slicing and dicing' toxic loans and mixing them with what appeared to be healthy loans. Several thousands mortgages were mingled together to form a Mortgage Backed Security, and then several hundred MBS packages were grouped into other securities known as Collateralised Debt Obligations. These were then sold around the world as pieces of paper that allowed wealthy investors to collect an 'income stream' without the bother of lifting a finger in human labour.

As these CDOs were so complex, investors paid ratings agencies such as Moody's to assess whether the CDOs should have had an AAA rating (very secure) or lower. The only problem was that the biggest customers of Moody's were often the very investment banks who issued the Collateralised Debt Obligations. Today, the result of this utter madness has been laid bare. A study by Morgan Stanley revealed that of the $450 billion worth of CDOs issued between the end of 2005 and mid 2007, there were defaults to the tune of €305 billion.[34] And the buyers of these securities were often hedge funds.

A hedge fund is a gambling pool for very rich investors who wish to escape taxation and regulation. Typically, you will need to invest $1 million to get into the fund, and the total assets commonly amount to €1 billion. The fund may have a registered office in Mayfair in London, or Greenwich Village in New York. It might be administered in Dublin but, to avoid tax, it will often be legally registered in the Cayman Islands. The fund managers charge their wealthy clients fees of 2 per cent a year, plus a 20 per cent cut on profits made.

Although hedge funds may have assets of €1 billion, they will use this as leverage to borrow much more, and then engage in more extensive speculative activities.[35] By mid-2006, it was estimated that 8,000 of these hedge funds controlled assets worth nearly $1.5 trillion.[36] And one of their favourite pastimes was buying CDOs, which they assumed would bring them high income streams because of the magic of financial engineering.

Few will cry for the losses incurred by hedge funds. But, unfortunately, their destructive activities are not confined to the wealthy. Up to the 1970s, pension funds were normally invested in government bonds to guarantee security. But with rising inflation, many started to invest in stocks and shares as well. By the 1990s, the explosion of finance led to a further liberalisation of pension funds which allowed them to invest in hedge funds. Though estimates vary, up to 20 per cent of European and American pension funds, and 40 per cent of Japanese pension funds, are thought to have been invested in hedge funds.[37] As the hedge fund managers get a 20 per cent cut on profits, and do not suffer individual loss when they lose other people's money, they have little compunction about going for high-yield risks. As a result, the pensions of many workers have also been liquidated in this absurd orgy of greed.

So good were the profits from speculation that the banks created Special Investment Vehicles, and launched their own hedge funds to create a shadow banking system with their borrowings, which were conveniently held 'off balance sheet'. One advantage of this was that they could evade any requirement to maintain a special reserve for the funds they lent out. Goldman Sachs Asset Management, for example, was reported in 2006 to be one of the largest hedge funds, with about $21 billion in capital. Its 'private equity arm', which specialised in stripping non-financial corporations of their assets, was involved in deals worth €51 billion.[38]

The orgy of speculation was supported by a new ideology which spread among the wealthy from the 1980s on: the shareholder value movement. In managerial literature, a distinction is made between the 'managerial revolution', which developed in the post-war era, and the 'shareholder value movement' of recent decades.[39] In the former period, corporations were supposed to have employed a governance principle of 'retain and re-invest' i.e. retaining people they employed, and re-investing in physical capital and human resources. But then, according to a common narrative in this literature, a group of US financial economists developed a critique of this model based on 'agency theory'.[40] According to this critique, managers of large firms were not sufficiently disciplined by the market and, therefore, did not allocate corporate resources in ways that were beneficial to the real owners – the shareholders. A freer capital market, it was argued, could more directly subject managers to market forces by making stock performance the benchmark for the allocation of capital.[41]

'Those whom the Gods wish to destroy, they first make mad.' This sums up the mania that overcame the global capitalist class from the 1990s onwards. Many came to believe that annual gains in stock performance should be in excess of 20 per cent – no matter what was happening in the real economy. The Chief Executive Officers of corporations were judged by their ability to hit this target, and were duly 'incentivised' through stock options. This way, they had a direct interest in following stock market performance. The whip came with the threat of takeover if the stock performance did not improve. The 'shareholder value' movement was a desperate attempt to raise profit rates, and, if that failed, to dispense a growing proportion of profits to dividend holders. This ideology had *real* impacts. It led, for example, to greater payouts for shareholders as they demanded higher dividends. In the US, the dividends to after-tax profits jumped from an average of 39 per cent in the 1960s, to 62 per cent in the period 2000-2006.[42]

It also led to the strange practice of companies buying back their own stock. The French company Danone, for example, no longer simply made yoghurt but has also engaged in speculation.

It bought back 31 million of its own shares in the past five years at a cost of €4 billion to help push up their price. The second largest company in the world is Exxon Mobil. It has also played the same game, spending a grand total of €108 billion on buying its own shares between 2001 and 2008.[43] Just as some shady pop stars purchased their own CDs to push themselves up the album charts, these corporations sought to increase their hits on the stock exchanges. It neatly illustrated how speculation is an intrinsic part of the system and there is no fine line between 'greedy speculators' and good clean capitalists.

A Mad, Mad World

The scale of the speculative activity that arose from the activities of both financial and non-financial companies was truly awesome. By the time of the 2008 crash, there was a veritable jungle of speculation. The much-cited instruments for such activity included:

Stocks and Shares

These are simply pieces of paper that grant a share of profits. But these pieces of paper themselves can become the object of speculative activity. In other words, bets were taken – not just on how much profit each share would generate, but on how the price of shares can rise or fall. In 1975, 19 million stocks were traded daily on the New York Stock Exchange. Today, 1,600 million stocks are traded daily, valued at $60 billion. On average, stocks are held for just one year, as there is a ceaseless search for ever higher speculative value.[44]

Currency

Corporations need to buy and sell currencies in order to facilitate trade. But, once again, currency can also become an object of speculation. If you think the dollar will fall below the euro, you might hoard euros until the dollar falls in due course. It is estimated that less than 15 per cent of currency transactions facilitate trade, and the rest is for speculation. In 1977, $18 billion was spent each day on currency transactions. Today, it is a thousand time more – $1.8 trillion.

Futures

As speculative activity grew, each corporation wanted to 'hedge' against risk and rising costs by buying future raw materials or energy at designated prices today. But, once again, this mildly sensible activity became transformed into speculation. Today, only 8 per cent of the futures market is spent on real hedging, and the rest is pure speculation. So, each day, 10 billion contracts are made to take bets on the future prices of currencies, government bonds, interest rates or just about anything. Obscene amounts of human activity are wasted by speculating on items such as the price of Argentinean wheat in Japanese yen in the year 2012. The speculators have not the slightest interest in using wheat to make bread – they just want to bet!

Derivatives

A derivative is anything that derives its income from some other activity. So you can have derivatives based on shares, currencies, interest rates or again, just about anything. You can sell and buy each of these items or you can just acquire the options to buy or sell these items in the future. Derivatives are often sold in a totally unregulated manner, in what are known as OTCs or Over The Counter trades. The estimated value of OTC derivative sales is $576 trillion.[45]

Credit Default Swaps

These are a form of insurance against the risk in carrying CDOs or other derivatives. A certain fee is paid to an insurance agency to buy a CDS and this is supposed to cover the risk. This was often used by banks to get around the legal requirement to hold certain sums back in reserve. If they took out CDS bonds, they could claim they were fully insured, and so this was the equivalent of a secured asset.

One of the main companies involved in issuing CDSs was the giant insurance company, AIG. It sold vast amounts because it believed that the Collateralised Debt Obligations would never default because they were so cleverly structured by financial engineers. Here is how one writer described how the London office of AIG dealt in CDS bonds:

> Initially, at least, the revenues were enormous ... returns went from $737 million in 1999 to $3.2 billion in 2005. Over the past seven years, the subsidiary's 400 employees were paid a total of $3.5 billion; Joe Cassano himself (the chief of the office) pocketed at least $280 million in compensation. Everyone made their money — and then it all went to shit.[46]

Portfolios covered by Credit Default Swaps shot up from $1 trillion in 2000 to an estimated $45 trillion in mid-2007. It has become one of the biggest black holes in the speculative jungle.

Leveraged Buy Outs

The 1990s saw a wave of mergers, as huge corporations, such as Pfizer, for example, bought up Warner Lambert to forge mega corporations. But, often, these mergers were driven by 'leveraged buy outs' whereby a predator company put up one-third of the price of its rival's shares and tried to pay off the rest by loading the company it purchased with debts. In 2007, there was another frenzy of mergers and acquisitions, with $3 trillion spent on buying shares of other companies. According to the *Wall Street Journal*, 20 per cent of companies who issued new shares are so saddled down with debt that they might be literally worthless.[47] Leveraged buy outs have become a bizarre game, whereby speculative capital seizes weak companies and tears them to pieces. As *Business Week* put it, the aim is to 'Buy it, Strip it and then Flip it.'[48]

This speculative jungle had an important effect on the transformation of modern capitalism. More and more of its activities were diverted into unproductive investment, rather than investment in the real economy. In the 1960s, about 15 per cent of the profits of corporate America came from finance but, by the early twenty-first century, this had risen to 40 per cent.

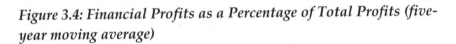

Figure 3.4: Financial Profits as a Percentage of Total Profits (five-year moving average)

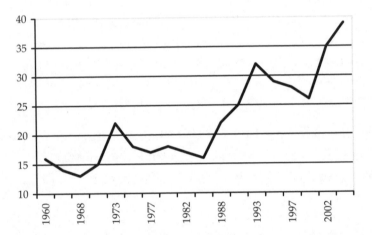

Source: Table B-91. Corporate Profits by Industry, 1959–2007, Economic Report of the President, 2008.

The explosion of this wasteful parasitical activity was not, however, just caused by the greed of a few bankers. Its deeper root is the decline of a for-profit social system. When the rate of profit drops, corporations will naturally seek ways to restore it by reducing wage costs and by diverting funds into speculation in the desperate hope of increased returns. Even if they partially succeed in restoring profit rates in the real economy, some will become so addicted to the higher rates in the fictitious economy that they will continue with speculative activity. Capitalism is guided by only one injunction – to make profit – and it matters little whether it is from producing real or imaginary goods.

Marx spotted the pattern some time ago when he wrote:

> If the rate of profit falls, the individual capitalist (will) drive down the individual value of his own particular commodities below their average social value, by using better methods, etc. and thus make a surplus profit at the given market price; on the other hand, we have swindling and the general promotion of swindling by recourse to frenzied ventures with new methods of production, new investments of capital, new adventures, all for the sake of securing a shred of extra profit which is independent of the general average and rises above it.[49]

For a decade and a half now, the conjuror's trick appeared to work, and capitalism seemed to have overcome its difficulties. The opening up of China by the multinational corporations allowed them to make huge profits. The 'savings' drawn from the super-exploitation of the Chinese working class were transferred to the US in the form of bonds held by the Chinese government and repatriations by US multinationals. The vast 'savings' were used to push debt onto a US working class, whose wages had long been held down. Debt-induced consumer spending then helped to ease the problems of over-production, and gave bankers a new foundation to open a new casino economy where all kinds of swindlers played.

Today, the solutions have fallen apart and the system has entered its greatest depression since the 1930s. Eventually, the huge social suffering may create conditions for a 'clearing out' of the system. In the past, the system has been revived through a form of economic cannibalism – where the survivors gobble up their rivals and gain extra advantage to re-start the motors of profit. The problem today, however, is that the corporations have become so large that the collapse of some of the large ones can open a black hole for others to follow. The spectacular bail out that started after Lehman Brothers fell is testimony to that fear. Instead of a sustained revival, we are, therefore, in for a long period of stagnation and social suffering.

Endnotes

---

[1] C. Harman, *Capitalism's New Crisis* (London: Socialist Worker, 2008), p. 10.

[2] R. Brenner, 'The Economy in Trouble', *Solidarity*, 29 January 2009.

[3] M. Wolf, *Fixing Global Finance* (New Haven: Yale University Press, 2009), p. 49.

[4] 'Beyond the Bubble', *The Economist*, 20 July 2002, p. 9.

[5] 'Corporates are Driving the Global Saving Glut', JP Morgan Securities, 24 June 2005.

[6] K. Marx, *Capital* Vol. 1 (Harmondsworth: Penguin, 1976), p. 342.

[7] Ibid, p. 406.

[8] Ibid, p. 926.

[9] Ibid, p. 874.

[10] Ibid, p. 280.

[11] K. Marx, *Capital* Volume 3 (Harmondsworth; Penguin, 1981), p. 367.

[12] V. Tanzi and L. Schknecht, *Public Spending the in the 20th Century: A Global Perspective* (Cambridge; Cambridge University Press, 2000) p. 5.

[13] R. Brenner, *The Economics of Global Turbulence* (London: Verso, 2006); G. Dumeneil and D. Levy, The Profit Rate: Where and How Much did it Fall? Did it Recover (USA 1948-1997) CEPREMAP-ENS May 2005; F. Moseley, 'The Rate of Profit and the Future of Capitalism', *Review of Radical Political Economics*, December 1997; C. Harman, 'The Rate of Profit and the World Today', *International Socialism Journal*, No. 115, July 2007.

[14] IMF *World Economic Outlook 2006* (IMF Washington, 2006), p. 165.

[15] L Mishel, J. Bernstein and S. Allegretto, *The State of Working America 2008/2009* (Ithaca: Cornell University Press, 2009), Table 3.2.

[16] Ibid, p. 47.

[17] F. Jaumotte and I. Tytell, 'How Has the Globalization of Labour affected Labor Incomes in Advanced Countries', IMF Working Paper WP/07/298, p. 9.

[18] E. Wolff, 'What is Behind the Rise in Profitability in the US in the 1980s and 1990s?' *Cambridge Journal of Economics*, Vol. 27, No. 4., pp. 479-499.

[19] F. Moseley, 'The Rate of Profit and the Future of Capitalism', May 1997 www.mtholyoke.edu/~fmoseley/RRPE.html.

[20] G. Dumeneil and D. Levy, The Profit rate: When and How Much Did it fall' Did it recover? (USA 1948-1997) www.jourdan.ens.fr/levy 2002.

[21] IMF, Statistical Annex, World Economic Outlook, October 2008, Table A3.

[22] J. Bellamy Foster, 'The Financialization of Capitalism' *Monthly Review*, April 2008.

[23] M. Li, *The Rise of China and the Demise of the Capitalist World Economy* (London: Pluto Press, 2008).

[24] S. Roach, 'How global labor arbitrage will shape the world economy' Global Agenda 2005 edition.

[25] M. Hart Landsberg and P. Burkett, 'China, Capitalist Accumulation and Labor', *Monthly Review*, May 2007.

[26] Ibid.

[27] M. Wolf, *Fixing Global Finance*, p. 69.

[28] Wolf, *Fixing Global Finance*, p. 112.

[29] 'The global housing boom', *The Economist* 16 June 2005.

[30] Board of Governors, US Federal Reserve Board, Household Debt and Financial Obligations Ratio, www.federalreserve.gov/releases/householddebt/.

[31] M. Cullen, J. Kelly, G. Phelan, 'The Impact of Asset Price Trends on Irish Households', *Central Bank Quarterly Bulletin*, July 2008, pp. 70-84.

[32] F. Magdoff, 'The Explosion of Debt and Speculation', *Monthly Review*, November 2006.

[33] Ibid.

[34] 'Insight: Time to expose these CDOs', *Financial Times*, 26 February 2009.

[35] D.MacKenzie, 'An Address in Mayfair', *London Review of Books*, 4 December 2008.

[36] R. Blackburn, 'Finance and the Fourth Dimension', *New Left Review* 39, May-June 2006.

[37] F. Stewart, Pension Fund Investment in Hedge Funds, OECD Working Paper on Insurance and Private Pension No 12 (OECD Paris, 2007) p. 6.

[38] J, Crotty, Structural Causes of the Global Financial Crisis: A Critical assessment of the 'New Financial Architecture' University of Massachutes Amherst Working Paper No 2008-14 p. 19.

[39] W. Lazonick and M. O'Sullivan, 'Maximizing shareholder value: a new ideology for corporate governance', *Economy and Society*, Vol. 29, No. 1 (2000) pp. 13-35.

[40] See, for example, M Jensen and W. Meckling, 'Theory of the Frm: Managerial Behaviour, Agency Costs, Ownership Structure', *Journal of Financial Economics* Vol. 3, No. 4 (1976), pp. 305-360.

[41] W. Lazonick, *The Quest for Shareholder Value*, paper at University of Massachusetts, Lowell, 16 October 2008.

[42] Ibid. p. 5.

[43] Ibid. p. 35.

[44] J. Clotty, 'The Effects of Increased Product Market Competition and Changes in Financial Markets on the performance of Non-Financial Corporations in the Neoliberal era,' Department of Economics, University of Massachusetts, Amherst, 11 October 2002.

[45] Bank of International Settlements, *OTC Derivatives Market Activity in the second half of 2007*, BIS, May 2008.

[46] M. Taibbi, 'The Big Takeover', *The Rolling Stone*, 1095.

[47] Quoted in Magdoff, 'The explosion of debt and speculation'.

[48] 'Buy it, Strip it and Then Flip It', *Business Week*, 7 August 2006.

[49] K. Marx, *Capital*, Volume 3, p. 367.

4

FIVE MYTHS ABOUT THE IRISH ECONOMY

IN MAY 2008, BRIAN COWEN APPEARED before cheering crowds in his hometown of Clara, County Offaly. On the back of a lorry, to celebrate his crowning as the Fianna Fáil chief, he belted out a little ditty which he wrote about his father:

> Ber Cowen he is a TD, me boys,
> Ber Cowen he is a TD.
> He got Clara a swimming pool because it isn't by the sea.

In a scene that could have come straight from the Ireland of the 1950s, 5,000 people lined the streets to celebrate how 'one of their own' had won the title of Taoiseach.

There were some worries about the Celtic Tiger but the new Fianna Fáil leader was having none of it. He was the main architect of the party's victory in the previous year's general election when he promised that only Fianna Fáil could prolong the boom. So he told the crowd not to be swayed by 'an ill-informed commentariat' who preached gloom and urged them to accept the 'temporary adjustments' that were underway.[1]

These 'temporary adjustments' had about as much connection to reality as the seashore had to Clara. But this was not the only statement Cowen got wrong; he also exaggerated the gloom of the 'commentariat'. Far from the media warning of a crash, they continued to hype up the property bubble until the very end.[2] Far from being impartial reporters, two of the main newspaper groups had a direct interest in the continuation of the boom. In July 2006, the Irish Times bought the property website My-Home.ie for €50 million and three months earlier the Independent News & Media acquired PropertyNews.com. These newspapers also relied heavily on property advertising and were pre-disposed not to upset their funders. As Fintan O'Toole put it:

> There is no question that almost all of the Irish media for the last 10-15 years has had a crucial economic stake in a rising property market. Because property advertising is very lucrative and is a very important part of what makes the Irish media tick.[3]

Story after story appeared with the sub-text: jump in and buy now, or be excluded for ever. The tone was exemplified by the *Irish Independent's* Con Power. After attending a seminar of over 200 leading property professionals, he reported that 'the average Dublin house price will hit the €750,000 mark or higher in 2015.[4] In July 2007, *Irish Independent* columnist Brendan O'Connor wrote a piece called 'The smart, ballsy guys are buying up property right now':

> Tell you what, I think I know what I'd be doing if I had money, and if I wasn't already massively over-exposed to the property market by virtue of owning a reasonable home, I'd be buying property. In fact, I might do it anyway.[5]

Even after the slide began, there were frantic efforts to re-start the hype. In January 2008, *Irish Times* journalist Kevin O'Connor wrote: 'the faint-hearted agonise over buying, hoping that prices will fall further. But don't wait. Buy now, don't listen to the doomsayers.[6] His colleague, Isabel Morton, was even more forthright a few months later:

> We all got such a fright last year that we huddled up in the far corner of the field waiting for the sheepdog to herd us towards the gate. Well the property gate is open

again. Not quite as wide open as it had been before, but open nevertheless. So let's get moving. You can never buy at the wrong time.[7]

This sort of effusion and euphoria might be expected from property journalists but what about the more sober profession of economists? They play an inordinate role in Irish society, appearing regularly in newspaper columns and talk shows to offer wise words on the state of the nation. Yet, for all their expertise, few saw the crash coming.

Take, for example, Dan McLoughlin, the chief economist at the Bank of Ireland, who was frequently heard on RTE's Business News assuring the population about the property market. He warned about 'talking ourselves into a recession' and thought it was 'completely ridiculous' to suggest that 'suddenly in 2008 the economy will fall off a cliff'. It would grow by 5 per cent in the medium term and, while there might be some slowdown, it was 'difficult to believe that it will decline sharply in the next few years'.[8]

Or Eunan King, the chief economist at National City Brokers. He boldly told the readers of the *Irish Independent* that:

> The gloom about the outlook for the Irish economy generated by the downturn in the housing market is misplaced ... the conditions for a spiral down and a recession in the economy are not present. House building was not the engine of the boom and should not be the cause of a bust.[9]

He was also involved in issuing a report which predicted economic growth of 3.5 per cent in 2008 and 4.5 per cent in 2009.[10]

Or Jim Power, the chief economist at Friends First. In his quarterly economic report issued in 2008, he predicted that the economy would grow by 2.3 per cent.[11]

The most prestigious of all economists are found in the ESRI. They don't work for private stockbroking firms or banks but claim to speak for the nation itself. The ESRI does not just comment – it pronounces. Its *Spring Commentary of 2008* deserves quoting at length:

> For 2009, we expect a modest recovery. Against a back-ground of an improved climate and with the easing in the contraction in house building, we expect GNP to grow by 3 per cent and for GDP to grow by 3.1 per cent. The con-traction in investment in 2008 will no longer be present. Consumption is forecast to grow by 3.3 per cent and ex-port growth is anticipated to increase to 5.7 per cent. This recovery will lead to a resumption of employment growth. We expect to see an extra net 24,000 jobs created in 2009.[12]

Like Brian Cowen, they too expected a 'temporary adjustment'.

When scientists make predictions which turn out to be bla-tantly false, they normally re-examine the assumptions and theo-ries which led them astray. The historian of science, Thomas Kuhn, argues that such moments of crisis can produce a 'para-digm shift'. Scientists, who once thought they could predict, are later overwhelmed by moods of doubt and begin to question eve-rything when their predictions prove to be unreliable. Some even take to reading philosophy to inquire about the very basis of hu-man knowledge. But, eventually, from this moment of crisis, a new paradigm is born and science resumes its confident, system-atic method of hypothesis testing.[13]

Irish economic experts, however, are immune to uncertainty – even when they are found to be blatantly wrong. They issue the most precise predictions with all the confidence of a Pope, speak-ing from his ex-cathedra chair. If the predictions turn out to be false, they do not hide, blush or stay quiet for even a short period. They don't question their own assumptions, or appear to engage in any form of philosophical inquiry. They appear to think that their use of quantitative data gives them an authority that few other mortals possess. If matters go astray, it is only a matter of creating new figures so that they can be proved right again.

It is relatively easy to poke fun at such experts. The problem, however, is that the mainstream media is dominated by this new, secular priesthood. Like holy men of yesteryear who claim a special line of communication to unseen spirits, they speak to the God of 'market forces' and demand obedience. Even after the crash, they continue with the same mantras. (The holy men, at least, face a crisis of faith when they fail to spot catastrophes.) It is almost as if we were still living in the hey-day of Thatcherism as the same old targets are raised as scapegoats for public woes: unionised workers who demand higher wages; a 'bloated' public sector which is squeezing the life-blood from the economy; an over-generous welfare regime which encourages laziness and lack of effort.

Our economic experts, of course, do not describe their targets in this fashion – that falls to the sub-editors who write the headlines. A subtle division of labour, however, takes place. Under the guise of objective research and supported by titles and educational credentials, these experts use cold, technical language which urges 'adjustments' and 'corrections'. This form of rhetoric is necessary to convey an impression that they stand above the fray of social conflict, able to provide a bird's eye view on what the nation needs. Their reports and commentaries spin around the press release circuits and land on the desks of the political class. The aspiring politicians from Fine Gael or Fianna Fáil may share the same mindset as the expert but they lack the gravitas, so they take 'key facts' and quotations from the experts to 'beef up' the content of their speeches. Finally, the sub-editors get to work, blaring out the message in a language which all can understand: 'School scam: Teachers take ten thousand 'sickie' days' or 'Spongers: €25 billion paid to migrant dole fraudsters'.

Such is the process of modern Irish myth-making. Our understanding of the crash can be shaped by powerful forces that have their own agenda – they want the majority to pay for it. But to succeed, myths and justifications have to be created to deflect anger away from the powerful and here are some of the common ones.

Myth #1: Irish Workers have priced themselves out of the market – we need wage cuts to become competitive again

ESRI Professor John Fitzgerald is one of the most outspoken proponents of this view. In an *Irish Times* article on 'How Ireland Can Stage an Economic Recovery', he supported 'nominal' pay cuts in the private sector and argued that if 'cuts in public sector pay rates mirrored cuts in private sector wage rates there would be a very significant gain in competitiveness, with a consequential big reduction in unemployment after three or four years'.[14] A few months later, Garrett Fitzgerald, his father, was almost ecstatic. Under the headline 'Reduced pay could be silver lining', he claimed that a Central Bank bulletin showed that private sector pay rates were falling by 4.5 per cent in 2009 and that this would accelerate the recovery in exports. The message was clear: pay cuts are good for you because they increase exports and so help create jobs.

There are a number of problems with this argument. First, while Irish wages have risen with the boom, they can hardly be described as 'uncompetitive' if a comparison is made with other EU countries. Table 4.1 provides the data from the Bureau of Labour Statistics in the US. This is of some relevance as the US is one of Ireland's major export markets.

With the exception of Portugal, Greece and Spain, Irish wage costs fall well within the range and, indeed, are slightly lower than most other older EU countries. The OECD Benefits and Wages database tells a similar story, placing Irish private sector wages nearly 11 per cent below the average for the EU 15 countries. The EU Ameco database indicates that Irish labour costs are 7 per cent below the average for the EU-15.[15]

Employers in Ireland enjoy two key advantages over their rivals. First, workers put in longer hours than their counterparts in other parts of Europe. They work, on average, nearly three weeks more per year, through a combination of fewer holidays and a longer working week. Public holidays and annual leave amounts to 29 days compared to an EU average of 34 days.

Table 4.1: Production Workers: Hourly Compensation Costs (in US dollars)

Country	2005	2007
Austria	30.20	35.33
Belgium	30.05	31.90
Denmark	33.53	36.67
Finland	28.68	34.18
France	24.56	28.57
Germany	33.38	37.66
Greece	15.17	18.03
Ireland	**24.51**	**29.04**
Italy	24.33	28.23
Netherlands	29.58	30.64
Norway	36.97	41,69
Portugal	7.42	8.27
Spain	17,59	20.98
Sweden	30.12	31.85
United Kingdom	24.37	29.73

Source: Bureau of Labour Statistics: International Comparison of Hourly Wage Costs in Manufacturing 2007

Second, employers benefit from the lowest social security contributions in Europe. Employer social security costs amount to approximately 10 per cent of employment costs, compared to over 45 per cent in France or 35 per cent in Italy.[16]

It could be suggested that we have drawn an invalid comparison because we used the EU 15 countries as our reference point rather than wages levels in Eastern and Central Europe. The data supplied by the Bureau of Labour Statistics indicates that the Polish labour costs amount to $6.17 per hour; the Czech costs are $8.20 and Hungarian costs are $7.91. But if competitiveness means benchmarking Irish wages to these rates, then economic experts need to spell out the consequences. It is not a matter of taking a 5 per cent or 10 per cent cut but of slashing wages so that they become one-quarter or one-fifth of their current rates. Such cuts would increase suffering immeasurably and, it might be asked, for what purpose? If Irish wages were driven down to that level, then the same learned economists would ask: Why stop there, we are still 'uncompetitive' against Chinese, Indian and Vietnamese wages. And while we were considering this question, Polish, Czech or Hungarian employers would hardly stand passively aside. They, too, would join in the chorus about 'competitiveness' and demand further cuts to stay ahead of the Irish. This is a game in which nobody but the large corporations can win.

Figure 4.1: Average Annual Working Time (Hours) 2006

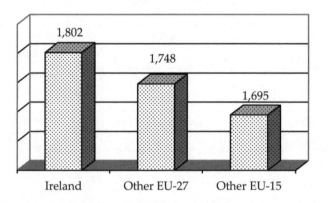

Source: Michael Taft, 'Farewell to Hard Working Families on Recession Diaries', October 15th 2007 http://notesonthefront.typepad.com/politicaleconomy/

Let us, however, leave these figures aside for a moment and return to the core argument, namely, that rising wages caused a decline in exports and, as a corollary, reduced wages will lead to a rise in exports and more jobs.

Exports are typically divided into manufacturing and services. According to the National Competitiveness Council, 'manufacturing unit labour costs have not changed significantly since 2000.[17] In other words, wages could not be the primary factor in determining the fluctuating levels of exports in this sector. Irish manufacturing exports have grown more slowly in this period but the main reason for this has been the fall-off in US investment compared to the first phase of Celtic Tiger.

When we examine specific areas this becomes even clearer. The two main industries which contribute to Irish exports are: Chemicals (49 per cent) and Pharmaceuticals (25 per cent). In other words, these two sectors account for 75 per cent of Irish manufacturing exports. Yet, on 2007 figures, these sectors were paying the highest wages, €19.85 an hour for industrial workers compared to an average of €15.11 an hour for all manufacturing industries.[18] This presents a certain paradox for advocates of wage cuts, especially as the textile sector, which does the least well in exports, has an average wage of €11.94 an hour.[19] It suggests that wages may not be the primary factor determining 'competitiveness'. None of this suggests that even if there is growth in export markets, it automatically translates into an increase in jobs. Manufacturing industry grew modestly in the period from 2000–2007, but employment in that sector actually fell.

The simplistic formula that posits that lower wages = more exports = more jobs, therefore, does not stand up. It is an ideological proposition in the strict sense of the term: a justification advanced for a particular social interest; in this case, employers who want more profits.

What about service exports? Ireland's services sector is dominated by software, financial services and business services and there has been a high level of growth since 2000. But, again, it is difficult to see how low, or reduced, wages played a major role. The first two – software and financial services – pay relatively high wages and account for 60 per cent of service exports. Nearly half of the 84,500 employees who work in financial services are classified by the Central Statistics Offices as 'managers, professionals and associated professionals'. The overall hourly earnings for the sector amounts to €25.14, and for the above category it rises to €33.66.[20] These figures are, of course, distorted by the obscene payments made to senior executives. But those who argue that lower wages lead to more exports do not distinguish between categories of staff and so their co-relation is further weakened by the evidence in this sector.

If the link between wages and export performance was not proved in the past, there is even less reason to suggest there will be one in the future. Financial services grew because of global deregulation and will, no doubt, shrink after the current crisis. They will be curtailed and subject to far greater scrutiny and so Ireland's niche position in offering 'light touch' regulation will be undermined. Even if workers in this sector accepted lower wages, there still would be little extra job creation in future.

A lot of service employment, particularly in Irish-owned firms, is geared to the home market and this raises still more interesting questions for the advocates of wage cuts. How would a wage 'correction' for a cashier in Dunnes Stores, or a hairdresser in Monaghan, 'help the economy'? Why will salary reductions for KPMG accountancy staff, who audit Irish company books, help bring more jobs? There is, in fact, every reason to suspect that it will make matters worse.

To see why, we have to return to the classic debate between John Maynard Keynes and the neoclassical economists during the last great depression. Keynes borrowed some of Marx's arguments and gave them his own twist. Nevertheless, it deserves summary as the mantra for the need for wage cuts is repeated as if this debate had never occurred. Paul Krugman, the prominent economist who writes a regular column in the *New York Times*, summarises Keynes's views well: 'Falling wages are a symptom of a sick economy. And they're a symptom that can make the economy even sicker.'[21]

Today's mainstream economists repeat the mistakes of their counterparts in the 1930s by assuming that markets correct themselves automatically, as long as no organised groups, such as unions or the state, interfere with their workings. Accordingly, they argue that the price of labour must fall in a recession - to balance an over-abundance of supply with weakened demand. Once wages reach their appropriate level, they claim, employers will feel emboldened by higher profits and take workers on and, at that point, the economy will resume again.

Keynes made a devastating response to this argument, explaining that even if wages were reduced, other items are required to restart production. You need access to raw materials, serviced work space, machinery – and these are not always immediately available. As wages are not always the sole or the main factor in production, wage cuts will, therefore, not guarantee extra investment.

Moreover, a fall in wages can either lead to deflation (falling prices) and, in that case, the drop will mean little to the prospective capitalist as it does not assist them in making further profits; or prices will fall at a slower pace and workers will suffer a real, rather than just a nominal, wage cut. But a decline in real wages means a decline in purchasing power and, if this is not offset by other forms of spending, total demand will decline. Where might other spending come from? Possibly from the capitalists who accrue extra profits because of falling wages. However,the wealthy tend to spend a smaller proportion of their income on consumption than workers do, who tend to spend more on basic items such as food or essential services. The wealthy are also more likely to save money or divert it into remaining forms of speculation.

Even if that were not the case, capitalists may not instantaneously make use of the increased funds gained from wage cuts. Having witnessed a calamitous fall in the economy, they are more likely to show caution before plunging into new investments. They also may assume that wages and prices will decrease further and so hold off making investments until these expectations are met. In addition, what sane company would increase investment in the face of falling demand for its products? For all these reasons, Keynes argued that wage cuts were more likely to trigger a spiral of economic depression from which it would be difficult to exit.

Perhaps we can escape this trap because we are not a closed system? Ireland is an open economy, which looks to the global markets for investment and markets, and some economists argue that wage cuts will put us ahead of the game. They are supported by a political consensus which suggests that, if Ireland takes more of this 'hard medicine' and does so before anyone else, it will be better placed to take advantage of the global recovery when it comes. The unstated assumption is that other governments will introduce stimulus packages to get their economies going again and the Irish will piggy-back along and then undercut them with cheaper exports. It is the same pattern of thinking that underlies Irish tax policy – the rest of Europe creates markets for US products and Ireland undercuts them by offering a tax haven. 'Look after your own' screams the cute nationalist, even while they are denouncing opponents of the Lisbon Treaty as not being 'good Europeans'.

This particular Irish solution to a global problem is, however, likely to run into considerable difficulties. First, a sustained recovery is still some way off and predictions about 'green shoots' are more than a little premature. These, typically, refer to flutters in the stock markets or momentary rises in retail sales rather than major changes in the real economy. Two economists, Barry Eichengreen and Kevin O'Rourke, have produced a number of figures to indicate that the depression is set to be very deep indeed, suggesting that 'world industrial production, trade, and stock markets are diving faster now than during 1929-30'.[22] State intervention to halt a slide into a deeper depression has been of a much larger scale than in the 1930s but so, too, is the problem of 'unknown unknowns' that have yet to surface. The exact scale of the unrecorded and unregulated transactions in the financial sector is still not fully known. Private for-profit investment will only follow the first signs of recovery and, if this is sluggish, it will be delayed further. Meanwhile, workers face ever more pay cuts as mass unemployment continues.

Second, the crash has led to a heightening of conflicts between states, impeding the co-ordination of a global stimulus package. One result is a rise in overt and covert protectionism. India and Russia have already raised tariff barriers, and in the first half of 2008 there had been a 40 per cent growth in anti-dumping cases.[23] Other countries look set to make greater use of subsidies to save their large corporations. In the US, there is also growing pressure to stop the 'export of jobs' and there are additional concerns about US public finances because of massive bail-outs. In a recent outline budget plan, the Obama administration stated that it would raise $210 billion in taxes by changing tax rules on US investment abroad. The target is a practice known as 'tax deferral', which enables US multinationals to indefinitely defer paying taxes on profits earned overseas by simply keeping the money offshore. Such a tax change would allow the US to recoup funds and deter further investment abroad. It could also choke off the life blood of Irish exports because 90 per cent of those exports come from foreign, and predominantly US, firms.

Third, once states like Ireland embark on a wage cutting strategy, the power of a bad example spreads. If US corporations can use Ireland as a testing ground for wage cuts, they are more likely to spread it across Europe. Already, for example, Opel-GM is pressing for wage cuts in Germany and the German politicians are conniving in this strategy. Others are likely to follow suit if they find that there is little resistance from unionised workers. Instead of helping to lessen the crisis, the Irish government's strategy can only make it worse.

Myth #2: We have a bloated public sector where pay and job security are too high

One of the most amazing features of the crash has been the way some members of the media have turned the anger onto public sector workers. In modern psychology, there is a phenomenon known as anger displacement, where an individual fails to deal with the root causes of their troubles. Displacement means taking out frustrations on people or objects that are less threatening. Rather than express anger in ways that could lead to negative consequences (like arguing with the boss), we instead express anger towards a person or object that poses no threat. It is almost as if Irish society has suffered from mass social anger displacement.

It did not fall from the skies because the employers' organisation, IBEC, has mounted a systematic campaign in recent years to attack public sector employees. Press statement after press statement was rolled out to denounce pension provision, the pension-pay parity link with current wage increases, and to demand cuts in public wages and social welfare. These attacks have been backed up by a set of spurious studies which have then been given prominence in the news media.

The relative success of the campaign is all the more remarkable because the public sector could hardly have caused the current crash. The trigger was clearly private corporations, both financial and non-financial, who engaged in an orgy of speculation. Many of the companies that IBEC represented, for example, speculated on land prices, stocks and shares, credit default swaps, future markets and anything that could bring in an extra buck. They systematically pushed their employees out of defined benefit schemes and forced them to rely on the same casino economy for their pensions. IBEC members, however, are not subject to public scrutiny in the same way as the nation state is and so it is easy to divert anger from themselves. Many citizens feel they have a right to have a say in decisions concerning the public domain, but do not, as yet, think this applies to how corporations use the fruits of their labour.

The most comprehensive review of the Irish public sector was carried out by the OECD in 2008. It noted that public spending increased 30 per cent between 1995 and 2005 but that much of the extra employment went on 'front line' service delivery, particularly in health employment (73 per cent) and education (42 per cent).[24] These had been dramatically slashed when Fianna Fáil leader, Charles Haughey, came to power in 1987 and made 20,000 public servants redundant. Haughey's cuts were so bad that nappies for incontinent elderly people had to be rationed. In the early 1990s, Ireland achieved the unenviable record of cutting more hospital beds per head of population than any other OECD country. Wards were sometimes closed over the summer to save money and cardiac patients waited a year for operations. After the Celtic Tiger started, spending began to increase modestly, but it only compensated for an exceptionally low level of public service.

Public spending, therefore, followed a rise in general economic activity and population growth and did not rise disproportionately to that growth. It was not funded by extra taxes or huge borrowings as Ireland ran a huge budget surplus until 2007. It, therefore, cannot be asserted that public spending caused the crisis in public finances.

The collapse in public finances after 2008 was directly due to a philosophy of trickle-down economics which assumed that if profits were high, tax revenue would flow automatically. During the boom years, taxes on capital and wealth were slashed and low pay rises were bolstered by cuts in income tax. The neoliberals wanted 'pro-cyclical' taxes which grew with a boom but they forgot that they would collapse if the boom ever turned to slump. So Irish taxes relied inordinately on indirect taxes such as VAT, Customs and Excise, and also on taxes on property. Although tax revenue trebled between 1995 and 2006, a full 17 per cent of that revenue came from property-related taxes in 2007.[25]

Figure 4.2: Ireland's Current Budget Surpluses/Deficits: 1995-2010

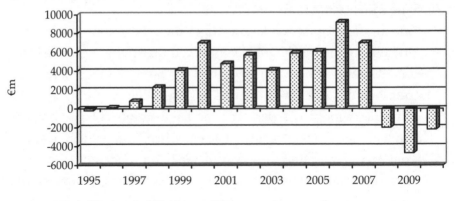

Source: CSO and Budget Stability Report 2009

Even when public spending was growing, it was at a slower pace than the growth in the rest of the economy. In other words, it did not keep up with population or real GDP growth. As a result, as the OECD explained:

> Government policy actually decreased the total number of public sector employees as a percentage of the labour force and decreased the overall public sector pay bill as a percentage of GDP. As compared to other OECD countries, 2005 data indicate that general government employment in Ireland represents around 14.6 per cent of the total workforce, which is relatively low among OECD countries.[26]

Ireland had, in fact, the third lowest public expenditure rate as a percentage of GDP, ahead only of Korea and Mexico. There are problems associated with calculations based on Irish GDP, but even if one uses a different measure, Irish public spending simply comes closer to average OECD levels. There is, therefore, no evidence to suggest that public spending was responsible for the crash. But do public sector workers have a more privileged position than others? The simple answer is that some conditions are different but they are by no means privileged.

One of the myths is that the public sector provides a 'job for life'. The reality is, however, very different as public sector workers are subject to the same disciplinary codes as other workers. Bus workers who insult passengers, firefighters who come to work drunk, council staff who physically assault superiors, can all be suspended or sacked. The state has also evolved a mechanism for keeping a large proportion of its staff on temporary contracts. It is virtually impossible for newly qualified secondary teachers to get a permanent job and most spend a number of years on temporary contracts. Of the 18,000 members of the ASTI, for example, 3,000 are part-time or temporary and 1,000 will lose their jobs from September 2009.[27] In the health service, over one in ten posts is held by a temporary worker and a high proportion of these 14,000 positions face redundancy in the coming year. Local authorities also recruit workers on temporary contracts on a large scale. Broadly speaking, about one in ten staff in many parts of the public sector are employed in the buffer zone of temporary and part-time contracts. The state tries to mimic the private sector in building in 'flexible' market mechanisms to let staff go when economic conditions deteriorate.

It is sometimes assumed that public sector workers do not pay for their pension schemes but those who have been employed since 1995 pay six and a half per cent of their salary to these schemes. The wages of public sector workers have also been 'discounted' to pay for better pension coverage. The Second Benchmarking Report of 2008 awarded public servants a pay award of zero per cent increase because 'A discount (of 12.5 per cent) should be applied in comparing remuneration levels in the public sector and private sector'.[28] In the private sector, employers have been closing pension schemes to boost profits, but where such schemes exist, the average private employee contribution is often around five per cent.

Finally, public sector workers are not over-paid and under-worked. They have a higher rate of trade unionism and have taken collective action to push up their wages when necessary but so, too, have bricklayers and general construction workers during the Celtic Tiger years. Different groups of public sector workers were successful in their struggles and others were not. Although ASTI got lambasted for taking industrial action, they probably helped increase teachers' pay in a subsequent round of benchmarking. By contrast, nurses failed to close a pay gap with physiotherapists due to poor union leadership. Other groups, such as civil servants, have been condemned to low salary packages over a long period of time. A higher clerical officer in the civil service in 2008, for example, starts on €24,255 and, after twelve years, just about hits the average industrial wage with €36,977. A business support officer in An Post starts on €22,024 and after fourteen years only reaches €36,087. In brief, there are a wide variety of pay rates in the public sector that reflect all sorts of factors, educational qualifications, market skills and levels of union organisation.

Why, then, is there an impression abroad that public sector workers earn more than those in the private sector? This has mainly to do with the repeated citing of a small number of studies which make deeply flawed comparisons. The basis of any comparison is the isolation of an 'independent variable' to which causal primary is attributed. To make any sense, groups need to be similar in some way, and one then needs to control for extraneous factors which might interfere with the causal relationship. If, for example, one suggests that smoking causes cancer, one needs to obtain a random sample and an equivalent control group sample. One also needs to ensure that other factors such as diet, physical exercise, or environmental risk factors do not contaminate the study. But this can hardly be done for two hugely diverse groups which do not resemble each other. It is like comparing apples and oranges, and deciding that one is superior in taste and quality to the other.

There are no private sector Gardai or prison officers, so on what basis does one claim that a Garda is paid more than an equivalent private sector worker? There are very few private social workers, so who does one compare their public counterparts with? We know that age and educational achievement have a bearing on pay levels. But if one compares two highly diverse groups, comprised of a variety of occupations, without taking any cognisance of education or age, one is engaged in a spurious comparison. Even if one does take cognisance of age or gender, one is still comparing groups which have an entirely different occupational structure. And this is precisely what some of these much-cited studies do.[29]

This is not an attempt to offer a defence of the bloated, overpaid managerial layer that has appeared in the public sector. During the neoliberal era, there was pressure to follow the model of the corporate sector and efficiency was supposed to improve through the 'leadership' of CEO figures who received CEO-style salary packages. University heads, for example, came to be paid salaries in excess of €250,000 in the belief that 'incentivisation' would unleash the sheer brilliance of their minds and inspire all around them. In the case of academics, 33 breaches in agreed salary scales were permitted as a means to recruit supposed 'superstars', allowing one UCD academic to get a salary of over €400,000.[30] Even when it was strapped for cash, the HSE found the resources to give Brendan Drumm, its CEO, a bonus of €80,000, although he already earned €360,000 in an annual salary package.[31] At the top layers, the notion of public service – that it was an honour to serve the public in a leading position without huge monetary rewards – has virtually disappeared.

As the public service shifted to an 'audit culture', where rhetoric about transparency was used to quantify and measure every possible procedure, new layers of management were added on. The HSE became the prime example of this 'USSR style neoliberalism'. The aim was to create a pseudo market within health where different hospitals could be benchmarked against each other through measurable 'outputs'. The time spent by patients in hospital beds for every conceivable medical procedure was calculated down to minutes and then 'benchmarked'. This, in turn, produced more paper work – and even more creative ways of filling it in to get the desired results. Like any command economy, the CEO could only issue top-down orders if they were supported by dense layers of management. This layer, in turn, are paid higher salaries than those they manage in order to assure them of their greater status and prestige.

While many, rightly, condemn overpaid management in the public sector, it is important to distinguish this from an IBEC-inspired campaign against public sector workers in general. IBEC has a wider agenda – to drive a wedge between public and private sector workers – by suggesting that a private sector employee has more in common with their company boss than with a worker in the public sector. By instilling this division, IBEC hopes to drive down all wages, for workers in both the private and public sectors. The attacks on the public sector have, therefore, become code for wage 'corrections' throughout the economy.

Myth #3: NAMA will look after you – at no extra cost!

The government's latest scheme to solve the banking crisis is the National Assets Management Agency. (NAMA). This is described as an innovative measure which will carry out the painless surgery of removing toxic loans at little or no extra cost to the Irish taxpayer.

The NAMA scheme was drawn up by economist, Peter Bacon, who wrote a policy document on the Irish housing market in 1998. In the interim, he became a director of one of Ireland's biggest property companies, Ballymore Properties, whose main shareholder is Sean Mulyran. This is the same Mulryan who was a regular attendee at the Fianna Fáil tent and a donor to the now deceased Fianna Fáil TD, Liam Lawlor. Peter Bacon was the European director of Ballymore and so it has been suggested, he is not linked to the company's operations in Ireland. But this is hardly relevant as one of the main strategies of the company was to borrow huge sums to expand in countries like Slovakia and Hungary, where he was in charge of operations. In Britain, for which he was also responsible, Ballymore was partnered with Michael Fingleton's Irish Nationwide. Ballymore and Irish Nationwide have a joint venture company called Clearstorm, to which Bacon was appointed director in 2003.[32] Asking an economist, who had such intimate connections with the property industry, to draw up a plan for cleaning up the mess caused by their borrowings might be considered somewhat questionable.

The plan drawn up by Bacon involves the transfer of loans to the tune of €80 or €90 billion to a state-run assets management agency, NAMA. (In these days of superlatives, there seems little concern about the difference between the two figures, but it is, in fact, €10,000,000,000, or more than three times the money raised from PAYE workers in the April 2009 budget.) NAMA may have to take on more than the €80 or €90 billion in loans because EU competition and state aid rules dictate that the scheme must also be made available to foreign-owned banks, such as Ulster Bank or Bank of Scotland. In return for the loans, NAMA will give banks a bond which will provide a cash flow that compensates for their loss of interest. Once these bonds have been issued, the state agency will become responsible for managing the bad debts. It can either call them in or allow them to 'work out' in the hope that it can recoup the money paid for the loans later.

The theory behind the scheme is pure neoliberal economics as the government's documentation spells out:

> The aim of establishing an Asset Management Agency is to provide the banks with a clean bill of health, to strengthen their balance sheets, to considerably reduce uncertainty over bad debts and *as a consequence* ensure the flow of credit on a commercial basis to individuals and business in the real economy. [Emphasis added][33]

In other words, before society can have credit, it must have banks with strong balance sheets. In the for-profit economy, we are totally dependent on the lords of capital and, if they do not make a sufficient return, we cannot expect any services.

NAMA has to negotiate on each 'portfolio' individually, and there will be no transparency about its dealings with particular loans. This is of some concern because, as we have seen, these have been taken out by builders and developers with strong political connections. Nevertheless, the government guidelines state 'information regarding its [NAMA's] exposures and their size is commercially sensitive so it will not be appropriate to disclose every detail'.[34] Only the total bond issued to each institution will be made known.

The explanation for how NAMA will operate is unclear but huge problems are in store. Say a developer borrowed €500 million to buy a tract of development land. That land may be worth €100 million today, assuming that someone could be found to buy it, but that does not mean that NAMA will pay €100 million for it. If it did, the bank would be left with a €400 million hole in its balance sheet. Multiply that up by all the equally bad loans and the banks would all be bankrupt. So, instead of acquiring bad debts and their underlying assets for what they are currently worth, NAMA's starting point will be to figure out how much the banks need to survive. If the answer is €450 million for every €500 million of bad loans, then that is what NAMA will pay.

A somewhat different scenario was presented by Citigroup analysts.[35] They estimated that the state is most likely to take over the loans at a 25 per cent discount. So, if a loan to a builder was €500 million, the state would buy that loan for €375 million and then chase up the builder for the assets if it was not paid. But even at this discount rate, the write-down would see Allied Irish Bank make a €8 billion pre-tax loss this year, while Bank of Ireland's pre-tax loss would be €5 billion. They would then need yet another injection of capital – to the tune of €2.1 billion in the case of Allied Irish Bank and €1.2 billion for Bank of Ireland. But what private investors would put that much money into a loss-making bank? It would, once again, fall to the state to 're-capitalise' the banks. In other words, even with a 25 per cent discount, taxpayers' money will be bailing out banks even further.

The scale of the problem was evident in an interview with Michael Somers, the head of the National Treasury Management Agency, which is charged with setting NAMA up. Somers has reviewed the account books of AIB and Bank of Ireland and confessed that he was 'aghast' at the size of the loans advanced to a small number of developers.[36] He noted that there were 3,000 to 4,000 staff within the banks managing these loans but thought that NAMA would only have a small core staff of between 30 to 40 people to oversee this operation. He said that lawyers were already lining up in the courts for a 'bonanza' because of all the legal cases the developers might bring to delay or contest any state sale of their assets. It sounds a little like the saga of the corruption tribunals starting all over again and it is not difficult to predict the outcome. As cases will go on for years, NAMA will be blackmailed into going soft on the developers.

Even if the state gets over all the legal problems, it will then have to make a judgment call on what to do about the underlying assets of the developers who have taken out huge loans. The assets backing these loans stretch from Budapest to Ballinasloe; some are tracts of land; others are half completed apartment blocks or offices; others are completed but, if the state forced through a sale, it would get a negligible return. After all, who but another developer might be willing to take these assets off the state? This is a scenario that is discussed in Peter Bacon's original plan, in a somewhat oblique way:

> Many of the impaired assets will be capable of achieving higher values if they can be worked out rather than disposed. A key issue to successful work out will be

access to additional funds … required for the work out. It is extremely difficult to see how the existing property developers will be able to access capital markets … and the banks' capacity to extend credit will be limited by the absence of collateral available to them.

An Asset Management Company would be able to achieve project oversight.… If properly structured and resourced (with relevant property-related skills) such an entity would have the potential to attract long-term capital in a manner that individual development companies could not.[37]

The Asset Management Company referred to above became NAMA and one can, therefore, only admire the brilliant scheme from the economist turned property developer turned economist again. Developers are stuck with big projects which they cannot complete because they cannot get further loans. But if a state agency 'took project oversight' while being resourced 'with relevant property skills', then they could get moving again. It sounds strangely like a partnership where a state company joins with a developer's 'expertise' to 'work out' the loans. And all the while Irish taxpayers take on more debt, while the work-out continues and we await the return of the property bubble.

A report in the *Sunday Business Post*, which appears to have come from well-placed insiders, shows that this is likely to happen. The report indicated that 'the plans for NAMA include a likely agreement to protect the country's largest developers from being put into receivership or liquidation'.[38] It stated that NAMA is also being lined up as 'a bank providing finance to developers in certain cases where a project is stalled by lack of finance'.[39] As well as rescuing the banks, the Irish taxpayer will be helping to keep most of the top 20 developers out of bankruptcy.[40] This is really quite amazing stuff. The Irish rich have long regarded the state as their private property, and while there is some democratic pretence at serving the people, this shows how it functions as a servant to the needs of the wealthy.

NAMA will add a huge burden to Ireland's national debt, which currently stands at €54 billion. Rising levels of state debt allow international bond holders to squeeze out more in interest payments because they can claim there is a possibility of a sovereign debt default. The estimates of the extra costs of borrowing to fund NAMA varies, but it will be somewhere in the region of €1 billion or €2 billion a year.[41] That, it should be noted, represents a substantial part of the sums raised in the April Budget of 2009.

Myth #4: We have got a plan – the smart economy

It used to be known as the 'knowledge economy'. Then it became the 'information society'. Now it is the 'smart economy'. Fads and fashions sweep across the desktops of state bureaucrats almost as quickly as youth sub-cultures change. Today you will find IDA executives, tired and jaded politicians and local partnership committees talk the language of 'innovation', 'knowledge capital' and 'smart green technology'. It is supposed to be the key to Ireland's future.

At the end of 2008, the government launched its blueprint for the future, entitled *Building Ireland's Smart Economy: A Framework for Sustainable Economic Renewal*. This is the strategy for a post-Celtic Tiger Ireland, and it suggests that the country is aiming to become an innovation 'hotspot' or the new Silicon Valley of Europe. From the phoenix of abandoned building sites and the decline of manufacturing will rise a smart economy that has 'at its core, an exemplary research, innovation and commercial ecosystem'.[42] The strategy is based on creating a tight fusion of academic research and private industry, to generate a new stream of discoveries. Ireland's sophisticated intellectual property regime will then allow these discoveries to be rapidly 'commercialised' so that fee income and possible new technologies would follow. A particular research focus will be placed on information communications technology, biotechnology and green energy.

Serious efforts have already been made by the Industrial Development Authority (IDA), the Higher Education Authority (HEA) and Science Foundation Ireland (SFI) to move in this direction in a coordinated way. Alongside the effusive business-speak that drips out of government publications, resources and funds were made available to implement a change of development strategy during the boom years. Considerable sums have been invested in science and technology, employing researchers, building new research facilities, and promoting a reorganisation of universities to align them to the direct needs of industry. The number of SFI-funded post-doctoral researchers has jumped five-fold and the number of SFI-funded PhD students has jumped eight-fold, from 120 in 2003 to 1,000 in 2007. One result has been a rise in the number of patents being filed by research groups. According to the IDA, 40 per cent of the Foreign Direct Investment projects they won in 2008 were in research and developments initiatives.[43]

But while this represents an important shift, there are severe limitations to the strategy and it is doubtful if it can offer a sustained way forward for Irish capitalism.

It relies on a quick-fix strategy of importing international superstar scientists, who become the Principal Investigators and form a research cluster around them. There is little effort to develop a scientific culture in schools and colleges which would generate its own scientific discoveries. A reliance on recruiting Principal Investigators, through high monetary rewards, is employed widely in the US, where vast sums are spent to attract talented scientists from across the world. It appeared to work in Ireland during the Celtic Tiger period, when there were also large sums for 'superstar' scientists. But there are also huge costs, as the best scientists do not always work for money, and those who see money as their prime motivation are often likely to rest on the laurels of past achievements. All sorts of games are played to ensure that big names are used to attract funding, but the real work is often done by others. Where, as in the case of Ireland, there is not a strong institutional setting that is independent of the 'superstars', they are likely to have even more leverage. As a result, the clusters formed in this very hierarchical model can be subject to high levels of exploitation.

There is some evidence that this is happening. Many universities have no observable salary scales for contract researchers. The scales are often subject to the discretion of the grant writer – usually the Principal Investigator who tenders for grants – and people with the same qualifications and experience often get different rates of pay. Researchers are used as cheap academic labour and pressured into a host of other administrative and teaching duties which are not rewarded. Job security has been denied, and a systematic effort is underway to deprive researchers of their rights under the Fixed Term Workers Act. Researchers are also denied pension coverage and rights to parental and sick leave. The overall result is huge dissatisfaction and low morale among the bulk of young researchers. [44] This does not bode well for becoming an innovation 'hotspot'.

The Irish state strategy is also based on a full endorsement of the corporate takeover of science. Intellectual property effectively represents a privatisation of knowledge and stands in sharp contrast to the traditional notion of a 'republic of science' where knowledge was shared and the for-profit motive was kept at bay. This tradition enabled scientific research to grow at a rapid pace as findings were pooled and openly debated. Developments in biotechnology and the resultant lure of money broke this down in the US and the model of privatised science has now spread across the world.

Ireland, however, has taken this model to an extreme, by connecting research institutions to the direct needs of large corporations. In reality, scientific research has become another hidden subsidy that is offered to these corporations, particularly in the pharmaceutical industry, to attract them to Ireland. Evidence from elsewhere suggests that a link-up with such companies carries with it significant danger for genuine objective research.[45] Research findings which are inimical to corporate interests can sometimes not get published, and there is often a high correlation between favourable reviews of drugs and sponsorship by corporations.

This is not merely a moral critique – it also has direct consequences for the current development strategy because the push towards a smart economy is being driven by tax breaks and tax tricks designed to attract US companies. Ireland is trying to perform the same feat with research and development as it did with the financial services. It is setting itself up as a location where it appears that more scientific research is carried out than might actually be the case, in order to offer reduced taxes. The *Wall Street Journal* explains the logic:

> The research facilities are necessary to satisfy Inland Revenue Service rules on moving intellectual property abroad. To do so – and thus have profits from it to be taxed abroad – a company must be able to argue plausibly that its offshore unit is at least partly responsible for the innovations. A common device is to take successful, patented American ideas and then develop new generations of them – with the help of the offshore research division. The ownership of the new version (and profits on licensing it) can then legally be shared between the US parent company and the offshore unit.[46]

This outlook is evident in the government's document on *Building Ireland's Smart Economy*. The core of the strategy lies in providing even more tax breaks and corporate welfare. The document promises, 'Highly favourable tax measures, including exemptions from corporation tax arising in the first three years of business start ups'.[47] Tax credit for spending on research has already increased to 25 per cent and the April 2009 budget gave additional tax relief for acquiring intellectual property. Viewed in this light, Ireland's smart economy is an extension of the same old story of offering ever more inducements to Pfizer, Microsoft and Google.

This strategy will most likely come up directly against the US government's current efforts to crack down on tax havens. Although the corporation tax rate in the US is set at 35 per cent, its corporations only pay an effective tax rate of 2.3 per cent. In a country that is now strapped for cash and facing growing pressure to 'stop the export of jobs', the US administration is adopting a new rhetoric. Obama says he is now opposed to 'a tax code that says you should pay lower taxes if you create a job in Bangalore, India, than if you create one in Buffalo, New York'.[48] Read Dublin for Bangalore and you get the picture. As the *New York Times* put it, Obama's new proposals:

> ... would especially hit pharmaceutical, technology, financial and consumer goods companies – among them Goldman Sachs, Microsoft, Pfizer and Procter & Gamble – that have major overseas operations or subsidiaries in tax havens like the Cayman Islands.[49]

And not just in the Cayman Islands. A special report from the US Government Accountability Office has found that 83 of the 100 largest American companies have subsidiaries in tax havens.[50] And one of the tax havens it named was Ireland.

A strategy founded on the tax needs of large US corporations provides a very flimsy foundation for a 'smart economy'. The reality is that overall business expenditure on research and development in Ireland still lags behind the OECD average. Bluster about Ireland becoming an innovation hot spot, when the real foundations have not been laid in place, will hardly work. Claiming that Ireland can, for example, become a leading centre for energy research is absurd. There has been no serious tradition in this that is comparable to Danish research on wind, Canadian research on fuel cells, or French and Japanese research on public transport systems. While the current strategy may, or may not, prolong the activity of US corporations such as Pfizer, IBM and Microsoft in Ireland, it is not a viable long-term strategy for the Irish economy.

Myth #5: All together now – we need to share the pain

They never stop repeating it. We are all in the same boat, pulling together for the good of the country. Before becoming a Fine Gael candidate, RTE's economics correspondent, George Lee, did a special programme that went out just before the April 2009 Budget. Irish flags fluttered everywhere and the commentary switched between dire economic statistics and Irish football teams. A sports coach spoke about the psyche of picking ourselves up and becoming a 'winning team again'. The message could hardly be clearer: we are all in it together and have to share the pain.

This type of crude economic nationalism is supposed to offer comfort to the population who are experiencing huge social suffering, and it is entirely fake.

Talk of 'sharing the pain' stands in marked contrast to the silence about 'sharing the wealth' during the Celtic Tiger years. Then, there was positive celebration of the success stories of the Irish rich as if their allure could spread to the rest of society. When you read that Michael Smurfit's yacht was so big it could not pull into Dun Laoghaire harbour, you were encouraged to think that the Irish were ruling the waves. Patriotic hearts were also supposed to flutter when the Irish developer, Garrett Kellegher, announced plans to spend €1.2 billion to build the highest tower block in North America. The country's political elite modelled themselves on their mentors in the US and barely concealed their belief that inequality was necessary for progress. The legacy of those years is a profoundly unequal society, where there was not the slightest sign of sharing of wealth. A pyramid was formed where the top one per cent owned 20 per cent of the wealth. On the other end of the pyramid, about 730,000 people are in the 'at risk of poverty' category which is defined as having less than 60 per cent of the median income, and of these, 225,000 people cannot afford basic necessities.[51]

This inequality means that the different sectors of society enter the crash under quite varied conditions. Instead of a common rowing boat, some come in cruise liners and others in luxurious yachts. Approximately 330 individuals are worth in excess of €30 million and a further 2,970 have a net worth of between €5 million and €10 million, and another 39,700 have between €1 million and €5 million.[52] If there is talk of sharing the pain, then this section of society needs to first experience pain, before they could consider sharing it. But, of course, there is no political will in establishment parties to make them do any such thing. In the budget of April 2009, €2,786 million was raised from PAYE workers through levies, but only €133 million was raised from taxes on capital. The reason advanced for this enormous discrepancy was that, for 'technical reasons', taxes on capital were more difficult to implement and so had to be delayed. Labour, as de Valera once said, had to wait and take it on trust that others would share the pain. Oddly, however, there were no 'technical' obstacles when the payroll systems in the public sector were changed in the middle of a financial year to accommodate extra pension levies.

Instead of the sharing of pain, a form of gesture politics exists to give an appearance of a progressive approach to taxation. This consists mainly of asking upper income groups to pay a higher levy. The income levy is graduated so that you pay 2 per cent on incomes below €75,036, 4 per cent on incomes between this figure and €175,000 and 6 per cent for all incomes above that. However, this only means that the better off will experience inconvenience while others take real pain. A 2 per cent levy on the gross pay of a low paid worker means a serious diminution in life style, with less money for food, medical expenses or holidays. A 6 per cent levy for someone whose income is over €200,000 is inconvenient but will not be painful. Those on such income are also likely to have investments which benefit from a myriad of shelters to make their income more tax efficient. And the really wealthy people do not live on income, but on their capital.

The 'share the pain' rhetoric is, in fact, an attempt to 'share the blame'. The assumption is that 'we' all indulged too much during the Celtic Tiger years and got carried away with ourselves. We lost our heads at a great collective party, and now must suffer the hangover. Just as the Catholic hierarchy excused its history of sexual abuse by blaming the 'culture of the time' so, too, do Fianna Fáil and right wing commentators try to spread the blame. 'We', it is brazenly asserted, must take personal responsibility for what happened. Yet, those at the bottom of society had no say in shaping the Celtic Tiger and nor can the vast majority of PAYE workers be said to be responsible for how the Celtic Tiger was run by dint of how they used their small savings. Even middle income groups did not just 'choose' to buy property and borrow heavily to do so. The 'choices' of the majority were constrained by much larger economic and political forces which deliberately shaped Irish society so that it resembled an outpost of the US. The elites established the parameters and told the majority to choose between the options they set.

If many borrowed heavily, it was only because they had little choice but to do so in order to gain accommodation. If more than half the population took out private insurance, it was only because they were too frightened by the condition of the public health service. If Ireland became a car-dependant society, it was because there was not a public transport system that was adequate for their needs. In a market society, people responded like logical actors who sought to maximise their self-interest. But they did not change or control that society; they merely assented to its rulers as long as they appeared to provide jobs.

The sole purpose of the 'we were all responsible' approach is to obscure our thinking so that we avoid locating the source of the problem: a wealthy elite who promoted neoliberalism and the system that gave rise to it, capitalism. Once the causes of the crash are understood, the only rational approach to adopt is to oppose paying for a mess that was created by the powerful. Instead of obedience, we need an alternative agenda for change.

Endnotes

[1] 'Our leaders need a fundamental change in mindset', *Irish Times*, 23 September 2008.

[2] See an excellent article on the website Mediabite.org, from which most of the material below on the property boom is drawn. http://www.mediabite.org/article_The-Media-and-the-Banking-Bailout_679566551.html

[3] Quoted in 'The media and the Banking Bail-Out' Mediabite.org

[4] Ibid.

[5] 'The smart ballsy guys are buying up property right now', Irish *Independent*, 29 July 2007.

[6] *Irish Times*, 24 January 2008 Property Supplement, quoted in 'The media and Banking bail out'.

[7] *Irish Times* Property Supplement, 24 April 2008, quoted in 'The Media and the Banking Bail Out'.

[8] 'BoI Economists criticise doomsayers', *Sunday Business Post*, 3 June 2007.

[9] 'The game is up for Stockbroker Economists', *Irish Times*, 27 April 2009.

[10] NCB, *The Irish Economy: Housing Not the Engine of Growth* (Dublin, NCB 2008), p. 1.

[11] J. Power, *How Robust is Ireland's Foreign Investment Model* (Dublin: Friends First, 2008), p. 2.

[12] ESRI, Quarterly Economic Commentary, Spring 2008 (Dublin: ESRI, 2008), p. 1.

[13] T. Kuhn, *The Structure of Scientific Revolutions* (Chicago: University of Chicago Press, 1962).

[14] 'How Ireland Can Stage an Economic Recovery', *Irish Times*, 24 January.

[15] *The Truth About Irish Wages* (Dublin: UNITE 2008), pp. 4-5.

[16] Deloitte, EU Employee Remuneration Survey 2007.

[17] National Competitiveness Council, *Annual Competitiveness Report* (Dublin: NCC 2008), p. 56.

[18] CSO, *Industrial Earnings and Hours Worked* (Dublin: CSO 2007), Table 5.

[19] Ibid.

[20] CSO, *Earnings and Labour Costs, Quarter 2, 2008* (CSO: Dublin, 2009) Table 2.

[21] 'Falling Wages Syndrome', *New York Times*, 3 May 2009.

[22] B. Eichengreen and K. O Rourke, A Tale of Two Depressions http://www.voxeu.org/index.php?q=node/3421

[23] 'Barrier to entry', *Economist*, 18 December 2008.

[24] OECD, *Towards an Integrated Public Service* (Dublin: OECD, 208), Table 1.2, p. 22.

[25] Goodbody Stockers, *Irish Economic Commentary*, December 2006.

[26] OECD, *Towards an Integrated Public Service* (Dublin: OECD, 208), p. 21.

[27] ASTI Press Release: 'Schools will lose 2.6 teachers from September', 15 April 2009.

[28] *Report of the Public Sector Benchmarking Body*, 21 December 2007, p. 7.

[29] E. Kelly, S. McGuinness, P.O Connell, *Benchmarking, Social Partnership and Higher Remuneration: Wage Setting Institutions and the Public-Private Sector Wage Gap in Ireland* (Dublin ESRI 2008) ESRI Working Paper 270.

[30] 'Ireland's Highest Paid Academic', *Irish Times*, 26 April 2009.

[31] 'HSE Defends €80,000 bonus for Drumm', *Irish Examiner*, 15 September 2007.

[32] 'Just because Teflon is invisible when it is wrapped around the Golden Circle doesn't mean it is a figment of your imagination', *Sunday Tribune*, 19 April 2009.

[33] NAMA, Questions and Answers in Relation to the National Asset Management Agency (NAMA) initiative, p. 12.

[34] Ibid, p. 4.

[35] ' AIB, BoI to provide 60% of NAMA assets – Citigroup', *Irish Times*, 16 April 2009.

[36] 'Somers says NAMA in new territory with 'bad bank', *Irish Times*, 15 May 2009.

[37] P. Bacon, *Evaluation of Option for Resolving Property Loan Impairments and Associated Capital Adequacy of Irish Credit Institution: Proposal for a National Asset Management Agency (NAMA)* (Dublin: National treasury Management Agency, 2009), pp. 5-6.

[38] 'Nama: A Ghost of a Chance', *Sunday Business Post*, 17 May 2009.

[39] Ibid.

[40] 'Nama plan to protect large developers from collapse', *Sunday Business Post*, 17 May 2009.

[41] 'Ireland's uniquely steep slump down to us', *Irish Times*, 29 April 2009.

[42] *Building Ireland's Smart Economy: A Framework for sustainable economic renewal* (Dublin: Stationary Office, 2008), p. 8.

[43] SFI, *Powering the Smart Economy* (Dublin: SFI, 2008), p. 7.

[44] Trinity Research Staff Association *Contract Researchers in Trinity: A Frontline Perspective* (Dublin: TRSA, 2008) p. 8.

[45] M. Angell, *The Truth about Drug Companies* (New York: Random House, 2004) and S. Krimsky, 'The Profit of Scientific Discovery and Its Normative Effects', *Kent Law Review*, Vol. 75, No. 1 (1999), pp. 15-39.

[46] 'Irish subsidiary lets Microsoft off the hook', *Wall Street Journal*, 7 November 2005.

[47] *Building Ireland's Smart Economy*, p. 13.

[48] 'Obama calls for new curbs on offshore tax-havens', *New York Times*, 4 May 2009.

[49] Ibid.

[50] GAO, *Large US Corporations and Federal Contractors with Subsidiaries in Jurisdiction listed as Tax haven or Financial Privacy Jurisdiction* (Washington: GAO 2008).

[51] Combat Poverty Agency, *Pre-Budget Submission 2009* (Dublin, CPA, 2009), p. 2.

[52] Bank of Ireland, *The Wealth of the Nation* (Dublin: Bank of Ireland, 2008) p. 13.

5

A RADICAL AGENDA FOR CHANGE: THE NINE STEPS

A T THE START OF 2008, A 'SOFT LANDING' was expected, after which economic growth was predicted to resume again. However by 2009, Paul Krugman, one of the best known US economists, was describing Ireland as a 'worst case scenario'. Warning the US public through the pages of the *New York Times*, he rhetorically asked:

> How did Ireland get into its current bind? By being just like us, only more so. Like its near-namesake Iceland, Ireland jumped with both feet into the brave new world of unsupervised global markets.[1]

A radical change of direction is needed and practical solutions are required that offer a way out of the crisis.

In framing such solutions, our primary concern must be the relief of the majority from social suffering. This represents a break from the current official thinking which asks: How do we prop up a business elite even though they helped cause the mess? Fianna Fáil ministers, such as Noel Dempsey, may occasionally use radical rhetoric and describe some of the bankers as guilty of 'economic treason',[2] but the government strategy relies on supporting the same bankers in the hope that trickle-down economics will work again. It is necessary to break from this doomed approach. If workers are being asked to clean up the mess, it follows that their needs and those of the vulnerable in society must be paramount in framing solutions.

Radical solutions also demand that we step beyond the parameters set by a for-profit economy. As long as profit is the sole motivator of economic activity, we will have to revive balance sheets and dividend payments *before* an economy works again. This means that an even greater proportion of the collective labour of society will have to be given to corporations and investors before they choose to create jobs. Even if we do all of that, we can only hope that they have been sufficiently 'incentivised' by the lure of high profits to employ people. We cannot – under the logic of a for-profit economy – force them to take on workers or establish new industries and services.

The global crisis, however, makes us confront this strange logic and we should not let our thinking be dominated by mantras about 'competitiveness' and 'reducing public spending'. These are the very mantras which were used to marginalise alternative economic approaches and led us directly into the current crisis. In devising solutions, we should acknowledge that this is a systemic crisis which arose from a search for higher rates of profit. Those pressures led to over-production and a speculative wave of madness in the financial sector, so even if the system revives again, the same pressures will re-emerge in the future.

We need a fundamental change of a system that puts people before profit and growing numbers are seeking this change. To date, the people of Latin America have been to the fore in challenging the constraints of capitalism. They have elected presidents and governments who have promised to uproot the legacy of neoliberalism. These struggles have by no means ended with the elections and a process of deeper radicalisation is also underway. In Europe, a new revival of the workers movement has been developing for some time, particularly in France. This has mainly taken a political form rather than being rooted in local industrial struggles. Nevertheless, the shift in consciousness to a questioning of capitalism and a search for alternatives is serious and substantial. If there was a challenge to the for-profit system in Ireland, it would most likely take place against a background of other revolts or incipient revolts.

A shift from capitalism to socialism requires a dramatic political rupture, especially as the current global crash illustrates how every effort to reform the system has proved fruitless. This rupture can only arise from the workers movement, the key agency in modern society which has the power to re-organise society. A new society can arise when struggles over exploitation and unemployment escalate to such a degree that they challenge the current state. When we make reference, therefore, to the state taking measures to alleviate social suffering in the proposals which follow, we refer to a state that arises from these struggles and which represents an entirely different class interest to the present one.

Societies change through mass mobilisation and tumultuous revolutionary events. These produce a political break from the old order and the space to re-organise society on a different economic basis. But once this occurs, the economic transition from capitalism to a new form of society is often more gradual. While workers can take control of a new state apparatus and the main levers of economic power, a transitionary phase is also necessary. No society starts anew from scratch with brand new people who have not been marked by the habits and customs of the old. Bridging mechanisms are, therefore, required and the proposals below are an attempt to indicate what a modern-day 'workers republic', as James Connolly called it, could do to alleviate the current crisis.

Every solution, from no matter what quarter, advanced for solving the economic crisis involves a degree of social conflict today. Contrary to the impression given by supposedly neutral experts, there is no technical fix that can override the question, who will pay? Different social groups will inevitably advance different solutions that promote their interests. Business groups have already, for example, been extremely active in monopolising the airwaves with proposals for more wage cuts and extra cuts in their own PRSI contributions. Our purpose here is to advocate alternative solutions that might better suit the needs of the majority of workers and the poor. The proposals combine, therefore, a vision of what a different society might look like, with certain policies which can be fought for now in order to stop the majority paying for the current crisis.

Step #1: Stop the bail outs of the banks – create a good state bank and socialise credit

The bail out of six major Irish banks will cost the population dearly. According to Standard and Poor's, the international rating agency, 'the total fiscal cost to the government of supporting the Irish banking sector could reach between €15 and €20 billion'.[3] A study conducted for the International Monetary Fund put the cost at 13.9 per cent of GDP, or €24 billion.[4] The truth, however, is that no one knows the exact figure. The Irish state is taking over a huge level of bad debt and has no idea how much it can receive by selling underlying assets. More than a decade will pass before we get some answers.

However, the one thing we can be certain about is that the IMF's estimated cost of the bank bail out is higher than the total cost of the cutbacks in public spending for the next four years. According to the Department of Finance, the €3.3 billion cuts package of the 2009 budget will be followed by additional cuts of €2.25 billion in 2010 and another €2.5 billion in 2011, and in the subsequent two years there will be further cuts.[5] We can, therefore, assume that all the suffering that the people in Ireland will endure for the next four years will simply generate resources to bail out the banks. This is truly the greatest bank robbery ever perpetrated, only this time it is by the banks on the wider Irish society.

Why should we do it?

According to conventional theory, the banks are the lifeblood of the economic system. If they seize up, it is the equivalent of a heart attack as credit ceases to flow through the system. Every small shopkeeper needs credit to purchase stock from a wholesale merchant who, in turn, needs credit to purchase from the manufacturer who needs credit to purchase raw materials. If credit dries up, the chain of buying and selling in modern society breaks down. In order to get the credit system re-started, it is argued, the banks have to be 're-capitalised' with reserves so that they can borrow more from international money markets and start lending again.

The first part of the argument makes perfect sense. It is difficult to imagine a modern society that did not use credit to lubricate its economic transactions. But does it follow that the credit system needs to be organised by the very same bankers who created the mess? Even if they were sufficiently 're-capitalised' through a transfer of resources from the wider society, there is no guarantee that they will adopt lending practices that will facilitate economic growth. They would be more likely to adopt a restrictive lending policy which would constrain economic activity.

An alternative approach is to create a 'good' state bank and allow the existing bad banks go to the wall. A mildly reformist version of this approach has been advocated in varying versions by Joseph Stiglitz, Paul Romer and the *Financial Times* columnist William Buiter.[6] An Irish version of a similar proposal has been made by the UCG Professor of Economics, Terence McDonough.[7] Stiglitz, Romer and Buiter advocate it strictly as a temporary measure that is subject to later privatisation. They also assume that a good bank should be open to private investors who are driven by a profit motive. The proposal outlined below, however, makes no such assumptions.

The first step in creating a good bank is to recognise reality. The major Irish banks have run up such huge levels of bad debt that they are now insolvent or virtually so. A recent report from

Goodbody Stockbrokers (a subsidiary of AIB) estimated that the two leading banks may have combined loan losses of almost €19 billion. But since their combined property and construction port-folios include about €42 billion in loans to developers, and some of these may be worthless, these loss estimates could be conserva-tive.[8] In brief, the banks do not suffer from a cash flow or liquidity problem – they are, quite simply, broke.

The state should, therefore, withdraw its insurance guarantee scheme that made it liable for a potential €440 billion for the six major banks. This can be done by repudiating a costly measure that was introduced by a government which had close ties to the bankers. The government was misled by the same bankers about the true extent of their debts, and this is sufficient grounds for re-pudiating the scheme. It is worth pointing out that Arthur Cox, the company which was paid over €1.6 million to act as legal ad-viser to Finance Minister Brian Lenihan in drawing up the guar-antee scheme, was, at the same time, acting for the Bank of Ire-land, a direct beneficiary of that scheme.[9] The government should also withdraw from the current re-capitalisation programme, and recoup the €7 billion that was earmarked for Bank of Ireland and AIB. The effect of both these measures would be the almost cer-tain bankruptcy of banks.

The main losers would be the major shareholders and interna-tional bondholders. There are tens of thousands of small share-holders, but many have very few shares. While they might lose some of their investments, they were taking the same risk as those who purchased Eircom shares when it was privatised and lost badly. The big losers would be those who made large, serious in-vestments. In 2008, for example, there were 148 AIB shareholders who had major investments of over €1 million. These included such luminaries as Dermot Desmond, Gerry Gannon, the owner of the K Club, and Richard Nesbitt, owner of Arnotts. After share prices began to drop, other wealthy people such as J.P. McManus, Margaret Heffernan and John Magnier bought up AIB shares, hoping, no doubt, that the fortunes of the bank would be revived again. Beyond these major individual shareholders are a further 423 institutional shareholders, some of whose funds were set up for the express purpose of speculating. Irish society has no more obligation to support the funds of the wealthy than it has to support gamblers who lose money on backing horses.

The other losers would be the international bondholders who provided Irish banks with lines of credit for €150 billion. 'Bondholders' is a rather nebulous term for other bankers, sovereign wealth funds and hedge funds – in other words, a host of speculators who gave loans to Irish banks for relatively high-risk premiums. Before the Irish government guarantee came into effect in September 2008, they were charging an interest rate of 5 per cent for three-monthly loans to banks. The justification for such high rates was that the bondholders were taking a risk of outright default or impairment for the recovery of only part of the loans. As the bondholders already built in higher interest charges for risk, it seems only right that they should accept the losses that are a consequence of lending to bankrupt firms.

If these measures were taken, very rich people will scream and attempt blackmail in order to secure their money. A government that wanted to protect its people would need to move quickly, and in a decisive manner. Following the bankruptcy of the old bad banks, it should pass legislation to take physical control of the bank property and all accounts within them. This would be necessary to protect the fabric of Irish society from further economic damage. It should transfer all the deposits and healthy assets into a good state bank, which would henceforth administer credit for society at large. It should seize the assets of all rich borrowers who are unable to pay back the vast loans they used to hype up the property bubble. In order to reduce fears, the government should maintain its guarantee scheme for small depositors up to €100,000.

Such a bold and decisive move would have many advantages. Most obviously, the enormous costs associated with the bail out of the current banks would cease and those resources would be made available for other purposes. The re-organisation of the banking system would also reduce banking costs significantly. Instead of six competing banks, there would be one major network that required less office space, less staff and less money spent on costly advertising. Existing bank staff should be redeployed to other parts of the public service. A good state bank should also be led by people who take pride in public service, and not by those who demand ludicrous salary packages as 'incentives' for their dubious talents.

In the past, bank management teams have presided over systematic overcharging, tax evasion and speculation. The argument that we need such corporate leaders to direct us today is demonstrably false. A good state bank should be overseen by elected representatives of the people and representatives of the bank employees. Both should be willing to make available their personal accounts in order to ensure there are safeguards against profiteering. To break from the old culture of corporate cronyism, trained financial experts, who are willing to work for the average industrial wage, should be employed to organise the day to day running of a new state bank.

But what financial experts will work for the average industrial wage, our current apologists ask? Clearly not those who are used to inflated salaries, and whose primary skills lie in speculating and playing the casino economy. However, it is precisely such experts that we do not need. It is not a question of casting out a few figureheads for the failings of the system but of the removal of a whole managerial culture. By trained experts, we mean those who have developed accountancy, organisation and information technology skills to a sufficiently high degree to manage the day to day running of a new state bank.

The state also needs to outlaw any participation in speculative activities. The purpose of a good state bank should be to socialise credit rather than accumulate profit for the sake of accumulating profit. Socialising credit means paring down the primary function of banking to its essentials – lubricating an economy through credit. In any society, surplus funds will be created in particular industries or services that are not required for immediate investment or consumption. On the other hand, there will always be some who need an infusion of funds but who have not yet earned them, so credit may be advanced in the expectation that they can repay it in the future. Socialising credit means the organisation of this function for the benefit of society.

This implies prioritising the allocation of credit for projects which benefit society as a whole. If credit is in relatively short supply, it needs to be directed towards projects which create jobs or which help to create new services for society at large. So, credit might be advanced to small businesses or co-operatives which innovate and employ a few score of people. On the other hand, the concerns of lenders need to be assuaged as one of the largest groups of lenders in a modern society will be pension funds or the equivalent of the National Pension Reserve Fund. Instead of raiding the latter to put capital into failed private banks, the socialisation of credit means diverting these funds into longer-term projects which generate steady income streams, such as major electricity or gas generating projects.

State control over banking would provide huge leverage over the wider economy and this is why it is passionately resisted by the wealthy. It would give the state greater access to their accounts, and ensure that tax evasion and tax avoidance are minimised. By taking control of the land banks of insolvent developers, the state could engage in a proper housing programme based on real planning, rather than the chaotic greed-driven development of recent years. Repossession of homes during the current economic crisis could also be prohibited because, among other considerations, this would merely transfer the problem of ac-commodation on to other state agencies.

Two standard arguments are normally advanced against state ownership of banking. One suggests that nationalisation implies political control and that this leads to cronyism. In other words, that a nationalised bank would show favouritism to friends of the political elite, or would be subject to political pressures in its bor-rowing policies. However, cronyism is hardly confined to state banking. The AIB managed to fund Charles Haughey's lifestyle and wrote off the debts of the former Fine Gael leader, Garret Fitzgerald. The Anglo Irish Bank was deeply embedded in Fianna Fáil networks and, according to Sean Fitzpatrick, the secret of its success lay in lending to acquaintances made in golf clubs and rugby clubs.[10] Cronyism could arise from state control – but this also depends on the type of state that is controlling the banks. The current policy of allowing NAMA to manage the bad loans of de-velopers, who are friends of Fianna Fáil, is a certain recipe for the worst form of crony capitalism. But if there were a popular up-heaval in society, a new state would represent different class in-terests. If such a state grew out of a struggle by workers to re-shape our society, cronyism could be entirely abolished.

The other argument used against nationalisation is that ad-vanced by Alan Aherne, who moved from being an apparently neutral economist to working as a special advisor to Brian Cowen. He claims that nationalised banks would not be able to raise funds because 'investors would surely give the Irish market a wide berth in the future – not just in the banking sector – if the State undertook such an extreme step'.[11] This argument may be coun-tered in a number of ways. First, if the state did not lose €24 bil-lion by bailing out the banks, it would have less need to go to in-ternational bondholders for funds. Second, such credit is not al-ways desirable, as the current banks demonstrated when they used easy credit to stoke up the property market. Third, there is not one set of bondholders but, rather, competing interests who want to lend out money for interest. It would be possible to exploit the differences between them if some credit facilities were required. Fourth, the crucial issue, for all countries is whether they will allow themselves to be permanently blackmailed by the speculators who triggered the current economic crisis. If one European country which had experienced a social upheaval were to resist this blackmail, it would garner huge political support throughout Europe and bondholders might then learn that they are not the only ones who can wield power.

In making this proposal, it is important to distinguish it from a different type of nationalisation proposed by a group of 20 academic economists who state that in 'normal circumstances none of us would recommend a nationalised banking system'.[12] The Irish crisis is clearly so deep, however, that some of these former neoliberal champions now advocate state control. However, the nationalisation they advocate is merely a mechanism to prop up capitalism, rather than creating scope for an alternative to it. It assumes that the state will take on the bad debts of the banks and that a re-privatisation will follow in later years. The good state bank being proposed here, however, makes the opposite assumption. The bad debts of the private banks would be repudiated, and private capitalist control of the banking system would be ended permanently.

Step #2: Create a major public works programme

Unemployment is rising rapidly because of Ireland's great depression. In April 2009, there were 372,800 people out of work and it is estimated that 17 per cent of the workforce will be unemployed by the following year.[13] Even these figures may be an underestimate because a high proportion of Ireland's workforce are migrants. Under the Habitual Residency Clause, people who have not worked in Ireland for more than two years are not entitled to claim social welfare. The same applies to Irish people who have not normally been resident. Some of these people have been forced to join food queues at the Capuchin Friary in Dublin's Church Street, where, each week, more than 700 people stand in line because they are in desperate need of basic food items. This shocking scene is a terrible indictment of a failed economic system.

Traditionally, the Irish solution to unemployment was emigration. The country's past experience of chronic unemployment made it a 'storehouse' for the surplus labour requirements of Britain and the US. In the twenty-first century, emigration is returning again – with 30,000 people expected to leave next year in search of work. But unlike the 1950s and the 1980s, when huge numbers left, this will no longer function as a safety valve for the political elite. The global nature of the recession and huge job losses in traditional destinations mean there are few opportunities abroad.

The government will, therefore, be forced to deal directly with the problem of mass unemployment or, rather, it should if it cared about its population. But if the strategy is wage cuts to restore 'competitiveness', the government will see certain advantages to rising dole queues. By frightening labour with the prospect of dire poverty, it hopes to gain leverage to reduce wages. A different and more radical approach to the economic crisis would, however, look to a public works programme to alleviate suffering.

One form of a public works programme has already begun in a mild way in the US, where Barack Obama has inaugurated an $787 billion package to create three million jobs. This seeks to expand broadband internet access, to make government buildings more energy efficient, to improve information technology at hospitals and doctors' offices, and to upgrade computers in schools. It also aims to improve the physical infrastructure of the US and to facilitate a greater shift to green energy. However, despite Obama's rhetoric, the programme is quite limited. There is an over-reliance on tax cutting to stimulate private business and, as a result, the cost per job is far too high. Three million extra jobs in the US barely compensates for the numbers of people who are being laid off, and makes only a small dent in the total number of 13 million unemployed.

Japan has already spent over €6 trillion on its public works programme since 1991. Spending soared in the 1990s as Japan entered a long period of stagnation, was then reduced in 2000, but resumed again following the latest crisis. Much of the spending was on large construction projects which were often spread out over long periods. A report from Japan's Institute for Local Government, however, found that every one trillion yen spent on social services, like care for the elderly, added 1.64 trillion yen in growth. Financing for schools and education delivered an even bigger boost of 1.74 trillion yen, the report found.[14]

Public works programmes can have a beneficial but limited effect in a capitalist society. If they are based on tax breaks for business, as Obama has done, there is no guarantee about the predicted level of job creation because it depends on the willingness of private capital to invest. In a different type of society, a public works programme would be employed as an emergency measure to create the maximum number of jobs at the lowest cost. Instead of an exclusive focus on large infrastructure programmes, support would also be given to other labour-intensive projects which provide jobs on the average industrial wage. These might include projects to compensate for deficiencies in healthcare or care of the elderly.

The state could embark on a public works programme by creating a state construction agency which took on unemployed workers directly. Such an agency would eliminate the practice of cost over-runs which have become a pattern in Irish construction industry when private companies tender for state projects. This agency might be formed by the consolidation of construction companies who have been bankrupted by the economic crisis, and by the creation of local authority direct building units.

The distortion of the Irish economy by the property boom meant that 13 per cent of the labour force was once employed as construction workers. This is an undesirable situation but, unfortunately, its legacy cannot be eliminated overnight as change will require the re-training of construction workers to allow them to access new skills. In the immediate future, however, a public works programme should include a relatively high level of construction activity as well as other social projects. Possible projects might include some of the following:

- **Upgrading the rail network for freight and the public transport system.** The two Luas lines in Dublin need to be joined up, and the networks need to be extended to the outer suburbs. The abolition of the CIE freight service was an act of social vandalism that needs to be rectified. Upgrading public transport would help offset fines incurred by the increased carbon emissions caused by cars. Before the crash, carbon emissions in Ireland were running at 27 per cent above the 1990 Kyoto baseline level, even though the permitted level was only 13 per cent. The government was forced to buy carbon credits to offset this surplus and this was rising to nearly €200 million a year. Building a proper public transport system would, therefore, reduce costs in the long term.

- **A housing insulation programme to reduce energy usage.** Ireland's housing stock is poorly insulated because there were no proper building regulations before 1991. About 75 per cent of the stock is pre-regulation, and, most likely, uses energy inefficiently.[15] The current government scheme to provide €100 million for insulation projects is merely a drop in the ocean and will cover an estimated 5-10 per cent of homes.[16] It follows the standard model of providing grants for house owners to contract-in private firms and will be more costly than it should be. A mass housing insulation programme undertaken by a state construction company and requiring smaller matching funds from homeowners would be far more efficient. According to the Department of the Environment's own estimates, insulation could halve heating bills and save the average family approximately €700 a year.[17]

- **A national network of state regulated, publicly owned or franchised crèches and care homes for the elderly.** The Celtic Tiger tried to construct a twenty-first century economy on 1950s-style family arrangements as the state assumed that it was the duty of individual parents to solve the problem of childcare. At a later stage in the boom, it gave tax relief and provided an Early Childhood Supplement of €1,000 a year for children under the age of four, but these measures were woefully inadequate in dealing with Ireland's expensive crèche fees. The Early Childhood Supplement has since been withdrawn and children who are aged three years and over have been offered free places in private crèches. But unless more crèche places are created, this will produce chaos and a rise in charges for those under three. The state should live up to its responsibilities and use a public works programme to establish a network of publicly owned crèches.

A similarly atrocious situation pertains to elder care, as HSE-provided beds for long-stay accommodation for the elderly have been systematically run down. In 1985, for example, there were 7,275 beds in geriatric homes but this declined to 6,135 in 2004, even though the elderly population increased. By contrast, the number of beds in private nursing home increased three-fold. In 2009, a shocking report from the newly formed Health Information and Quality Authority indicated that half of the public long-stay beds have to be replaced by 2015 because of health and safety concerns.[18] The HSE has, unfortunately, used this report to start closing down public nursing homes rather than first providing new homes. The agenda of the neoliberals who control this agency is, it appears, to create even greater scope for private nursing care. A public works programme should adopt precisely the reverse approach: it should seek to build more public units and staff them to the highest health and safety standards.

- **A network of primary health care centres.** Half of all GPs
  work as one-person practices and, in a report in 2001, the Department of Health recognised the problem, urging a shift towards primary health care centres.[19] But instead of building
  such centres and staffing them with publicly employed medical staff, Health Minister Mary Harney handed the project
  over to for-profit enterprises like Touchstone. A public works
  programme could build such centres and employ staff to run
  them. Once again, this would bring a long-term saving to the
  state, as fewer people would use hospitals and a more sophisticated system of preventative medicine might emerge.

- **Develop proper recycling facilities.** A considerable amount of
  Irish waste is dumped illegally as waste charges are quite
  high. In a deep recession, ever more people will feel tempted
  to avoid bin charges by burning waste or disposing of it by illegal means. A proper recycling infrastructure, created
  through a public works programme, would cut back on such
  activity and save resources in the longer term.

These are only some ways in which a public works programme could help Irish society and there are, undoubtedly,
many others. The key point, however, is to stop another genera-
tion being scarred by the consequences of mass unemployment.
That should be a far more important concern than bailing out
bankers.

Step #3: Take back Ireland's natural resources – use the wealth to build up strategic industries

Most people traditionally assumed that Ireland had few natural
resources and that this explained why industrial development
was slower to start than in its British neighbour. However, in recent years the full extent of the country's natural resources is coming into view.

The Petroleum Affairs Division of the Department of Communication and Marine and Natural Resources recently issued an astounding report which noted that there was a potential 10 billion barrels of oil lying off the west coast of Ireland. That amounts to at least a value of €450 billion, even on conservative pricing assumptions. Sizeable oil and gas deposits have been pinpointed along an underwater ridge known as the Atlantic Margin which runs parallel to the west coast. The Dunquin gas field which lies 200 kilometres off the coast of Kerry contains 25 trillion cubic feet of natural gas and 4,130 million barrels of oil. The Corrib gas field off Mayo may have an estimated value of between €6 billion and €50 billion. New gas and oil fields have also been discovered inland in the Lough Allen basin. In all, Ireland could be sitting on hundreds of billions of euro in natural resources, enough to fund top quality public services that can barely be envisaged now.[20]

The problem is that much of it has been handed over to Royal Dutch Shell and Exxon Mobil, two of the nastiest corporations on the planet. This process began when Ray Burke became Minister for Energy. He abolished the requirement that the state have a 50 per cent stake in any commercial project and that royalties should be paid. He also introduced a facility to allow corporations to write off exploration, development and production expenses, extending back 25 years, against tax. The Flood Tribunal subsequently branded Burke as the recipient of corrupt payments for some of his other activities. The former Taoiseach, Bertie Ahern, added further to the good fortunes of the corporations by cutting tax rates to 25 per cent and giving them full ownership of the field. Norway, by contrast, imposes a tax rate of 78 per cent, royalties of 52 per cent and demands a 50 per cent state ownership. These terms have given Norway one of the wealthiest per capita incomes in the world.

There is something extraordinarily odd about a population suffering savage attacks in income standards while so much wealth is meekly handed over to global corporations. One can only ask: might not these natural resources be used to create new opportunities to help the country out of recession?

There are some precedents for a more radical approach. In February 2007, Venezuela's Hugo Chavez announced a new law to take control of the last remaining oil production sites under multinational control. Corporations such as Exxon Mobil, Chevron Texaco, Conoco Phillips and BP were told that they could no longer control the reserves of the Orinoco Oil Belt. 'We are recovering property and management in these strategic areas', Chavez coolly announced.[21] On 1 May 2006, the Bolivian President, Evo Morales, also issued a decree assuming control of that country's hydrocarbons. Despite ordering his army to raise the Bolivian flag over refineries controlled by foreign firms, Morales's move was not quite as radical as some thought. Private companies were not expelled but were forced to accept taxes or royalties of between 50 to 80 per cent. As one commentator put it, 'many aspects of Bolivia's nationalisation actually replicate Norway's oil management policies, which are known and accepted by the global oil and gas industry'.[22]

Ireland could follow either of these options – provided, of course, there was a dramatic change in the political landscape. If the workers of Ireland mobilised and brought about a socialist society, huge possibilities would open up. A different type of government could make a careful assessment, on purely tactical grounds, as to whether it should impose full state ownership without compensation or allow a small minority private participation for a period in order to gain access to a wider skills and technology base. Whatever option it decided upon would provide it with a vast new stream of income to develop new strategic industries.

A publicly controlled oil and gas industry would allow Ireland to follow the example of Norway in developing downstream industries. Norway was originally highly dependent on the technological expertise of foreign companies, but then built up its own knowledge of extraction procedures, refining and supplier industries. Although it still maintains a strong farming base, the country has risen to become a technological leader in areas connected with the petroleum industry. This has further stimulated innovation and technological development in its wider industrial base.

With public control over Ireland's oil and gas industry, it would also be possible to shift ample resources into other areas of strategic importance. Instead of confining industrial development to one narrow stream focussed on natural resources, it would be sensible to initiate other forms of industrial production. Public ownership is probably the only way that Ireland can recover any standing in manufacturing and reverse its over-dependence on the service sector. There are a number of possible industries which could be developed strategically.

One is a generic pharmaceutical industry. The Irish workforce has some skills in this area as a result of the location of US corporations here. But just as the computer industry has begun to shift away from Ireland, there are also signs that some major pharmaceutical corporations could also start to follow suit. On the other hand, however, the industry is facing growing popular resistance to its policy of over-charging for branded items. When it attempted to impose scandalous prices for anti-retroviral medicines, which are used to fight HIV, it was forced to back down and allow African countries use the much cheaper generic drugs. Developing a generic drugs industry would run directly counter to the multinationals but it is what the world needs.

It is also possible to turn Ireland's present reliance on services to its advantage. If a sustained and determined effort was made to re-focus Irish health care onto a strategy of preventative medicine, new procedures and technologies might be developed. There is a popular sentiment in the advanced industrial world against an over-reliance on a conventional medical model. While some of this sentiment is driven by a rejection of corporate science in favour of more mystical forms of healing, there is also huge scope for technologies that promote preventative medicine.

These are only tentative suggestions and would require much more detailed planning. However, the approach adopted here contains two assumptions. First, that a manufacturing base is desirable, but it cannot be built up by a reliance on private capital. Second, there is a considerable discontent in many countries with the current economic order and a search is ongoing for new ways of living. A radical Ireland that re-orientated itself away from corporate America and produced items which were socially useful, could find new avenues for development.

Step #4: Redistribute wealth through taxation or confiscation

But where will the money come from? This is a standard question asked of anyone who promotes the vaguest of progressive reforms.

Ireland is now a wealthy country or, more accurately, there are a lot of wealthy people in Ireland. The problem, however, is not money, but a peculiar tax structure that reflects the neoliberal philosophy that has shaped Irish policy making. Ireland's tax take is one of the lowest in the OECD countries, amounting to only 30 per cent of GDP, compared to about 40 per cent in many other countries. Moreover, a disproportionate share comes from indirect taxes which tend to hit the poorest harder. There are two main reasons for this.

First, taxes on income are comparatively low because the government cut PAYE taxes during the boom years as a trade-off for low pay rises. While workers appeared to benefit, they lost out when they wanted health care or better classrooms for their children. The income tax cuts, however, helped their employers because it enabled them to give low pay rises in a tight labour market. The trade-off between tax cuts and low pay increases was managed through the active connivance of the union leaders in social partnership.

Second, the wealthy have a host of ways of avoiding tax or paying very low rates of tax. The much repeated propaganda claim that the top 3 per cent of income earners paid 33 per cent of income tax is highly misleading. This is in fact a classic example of state manipulation of figures for propaganda purposes. The 'income earners' referred to were what the Revenue Commissioners call 'tax cases', and so a married couple in this data can be a single tax case. If account is taken of the number of tax cases which are dual income married couples, the number of earners increase and earners slip to lower income ranges.[23] The figure also only relates to tax on declared income but, of course, the wealthy also live on non-declared income and capital. The Bank of Ireland's *Private Banking Report* indicated that the top 1 per cent of Irish society increased their personal wealth by €75 billion between 1995 and 2007.[24] Yet, the Revenue Commissioners assessed the total income of the top earners at just €4.7 billion. The discrepancy arises from the fact that the wealthy have found many different ways to avoid tax.

To benefit fully from Ireland's tax loopholes, you need to earn profits, not wages, and you need to possess capital, not labour power. The Capital Gains Tax provides a useful example. The Fianna Fáil–Progressive Democrats government halved this tax from 40 per cent to 20 per cent, arguing that there would be less tax avoidance if the rate was reduced. However, the one-time PD candidate Gerry McCaughey, along with his business partners, illustrated a loophole to avoid paying a single cent in Capital Gains Tax. Just before Kingspan acquired his company, Century Homes, McCaughey transferred his shares, as did his brother and another shareholder to their spouses. The transfer of assets between spouses attracts no Irish tax. Although all three husbands lived in County Monaghan, their wives 'lived' in San Remo, Italy. A few weeks after acquiring the shares, they sold them officially to Kingspan. Thanks to a double taxation agreement between Ireland and Italy, the wives paid no tax on the proceeds of the sale and the Irish exchequer lost €5 million.

This tax avoidance device may sound a little complicated and slightly inconvenient. So, the bulk of Ireland's wealthy elite have opted for the much simpler method of becoming tax fugitives. As long as they stay offshore for a minimum of 183 days a year, they are non-resident for tax purposes. The wealthy have access to private planes, helicopters and even jets, so it is difficult to monitor their entries and exits to and from Ireland and, to date, no-one has been prosecuted for faking non-residency status. Strangely, many of the wealthy do not move their families abroad but allow them to make full use of Ireland's public services.

The Revenue Commissioners only began compiling data on the tax fugitives in 2005. They discovered that 19 of these 'high worth' individuals, or 'hi wees' as they were known in banking circles, had personal fortunes in excess of €50 million. By 2007, the number of 'hi wees' had jumped to 440 and, between them, they appeared to control €22.5 billion in wealth. Ireland's tax fugitives include the two individuals who control most of the country's private media, Denis O'Brien and Tony O'Reilly. Other hi-wee tax fugitives include Michael Smurfit, J.P. McManus, John Magnier, Bono and Dermot Desmond; in fact, just about all the richest people in Ireland bar, unusually, Michael O'Leary.

Another massive tax loophole was revealed recently in the Anglo Irish Bank scandal. By using a device called a Contract for Difference (CFD), wealthy speculators could make a killing on shares without ever having to buy them – they simply gamble on the difference in share prices between one date and another. As a result, the exchequer loses all the taxes and duties that normally apply when actual shares are traded. When he was Minister for Finance, Brian Cowen proposed taxing CFDs, but then changed his mind when he was lobbied by tax accountants for Fianna Fáil's wealthy cronies.

At a time when the living standards of PAYE workers are being severely reduced, it is absurd to allow these tax avoidance schemes to continue. The government says they are closing off many of the tax loopholes in the current recession, but their actions are tardy and are not retrospective. In the meantime, the very wealthy continue to employ sharp lawyers to find other loopholes for them to exploit. In order to alleviate the social suffering of the majority, and to provide the state with sufficient funds for public services, a number of decisive measures are required to re-distribute wealth. Such measures might include:

- **Legislation to close the tax fugitive rule** and to require any Irish citizen with income over €100,000 to pay tax in Ireland or to risk losing their passports and Irish assets. These laws should be applied retrospectively to raise funds in the current emergency.

- **Removal of all property-based tax incentives.** Although these have declined since the crash in 2006, the last year for which figure are available, a total of €464.4 million was provided in tax relief to 19 property-based schemes.[25]

- **A tax on all income over €100,000 at a surcharge rate of 70 per cent.** This figure might be indexed to the rate of inflation to ensure that the vast majority of PAYE workers stay out of this rate in the future.

- **Elimination of tax subsidies on private pension funds for those on incomes over €100,000.** The gross cost of tax relief on private pensions was €2.9 billion in 2006, but two-thirds of it went to the top 20 per cent of earners. [26].

- **Restore the Capital Gains Tax to at least 40 per cent and close off loopholes.**

- **A sharp reduction in inheritance tax allowances on large businesses and farms.** Those who claim that their wealth is based on either the merit of hard work or 'risk-taking' should not be able to avoid inheritance tax.

- **The introduction of an annual 3 per cent wealth levy on all income-producing assets and houses, except the family home, for those earning twice the average industrial wage.**

The government has imposed a pension levy on public sector workers and other levies on all PAYE workers. Why not reverse this policy and introduce a wealth levy?

- **Removal of the subsidy for fee-paying schools.** Each year, €90 million is made available by the Irish taxpayer to private fee-paying schools. Parents who collect Tesco tokens to get the odd computer for their children's classrooms generously donate, through their taxes, to schools with private swimming pools.

- **Support European-wide harmonisation of corporate profits tax.** The 12.5 per cent tax rate has been promoted as Ireland's trump card in attracting multinational investment. But, as we saw in Chapter 1, it has triggered off a race to the bottom and a number of Eastern European countries are starting to undercut it in special economic zones. Ireland can either try to further decrease its tax on corporations or support a high standard rate of corporation tax across Europe.

- **Use some of the tax revenues raised by these measures to cut VAT rates and stealth taxes**. Ireland has one of the highest VAT rates in the EU, so it is no wonder that thousands travel across the border to do their weekly shopping in Newry and Strabane. Bin charges fluctuate but can reach between €400 and €500 a year. If we adopted the proposals above, we could cut VAT and eliminate bin charges.

Proposals to raise taxes always appear hard and uncaring, whereas advocacy of tax cuts looks soft because they are supposed to be victimless, yet nothing could be further from the truth. When neoliberals propose reductions in taxes on wealth, they never specify which public services must be cut back, even though there will be less money for them. It is perfectly valid, therefore, to ask them to state which services should be slashed. Should there be fewer teachers or longer waiting times for hospital operations? Should there be a reduced fire service, or fewer inspections on water quality?

As the country is facing an emergency, these proposals will need to be supplemented with more radical action. With so much economic destruction being caused, society has every right to confiscate the assets of super-wealthy individuals in order to provide basic services. If there has to be a choice between cutting social welfare and taking the assets of the rich to sustain minimum living standards, a decent society would choose the latter. In addition, the wealthy will also attempt to resist extra tax impositions, and so a policy of confiscation is the only sure deterrent.

Step #5: Reform the public sector – remove the corporate ethos

Our approach, so far, has been to promote far greater control by the organised public over the economy. If society is not to be at the mercy of the for-profit sector, it will need further nationalisation.

So, Eircom, for example, should be brought into public ownership to facilitate the development of a broadband infrastructure as it is a scandalous example of privatisation. When it was first floated on the stock market ten years ago, it was valued at €8 billion, and was entirely debt-free. It provided what appeared to be secure, unionised jobs to 9,000 people, and was investing strongly in the creation of a modern telecommunications infrastructure, something Ireland desperately needed. But, recently, a group of Australian financiers offered a mere €95 million for the company, or just over 1 per cent of what it was worth a decade ago. The reason is that the company has debts of almost €4 billion, up from zero in 1999. The workforce has been slashed to 7,000 and another 1,250 jobs are on the line. After ten years in private hands, Eircom has managed to connect only 23 per cent of all households to broadband. In South Korea, 93 per cent of households have broadband. Most of the countries that are considered Ireland's economic 'competitors' would be close to the 80 per cent mark.

The situation has become so bad that even Fine Gael are calling for its re-nationalisation.

Another area needing greater public control are the projects allocated to Public Private Partnership (PPP) schemes. Five PPP social housing regeneration projects in Dublin's inner city have collapsed because the developer, Bernard McNamara, claims that they are no longer economically viable. In other words, market conditions have changed and his profit margins have fallen. The hopes of working class communities, who waited many years for improvements, were shattered. This example indicates that projects such as schools or cancer care units, which have been entrusted to PPPs, can also be subject to market fluctuations. Even if this were not to occur, PPP projects cost more than if the state provided the services directly. The Comptroller and Auditor General found that schools provided under the PPP route cost between 8 to 13 per cent higher than the traditional route.[27]

But if we advocate an increased role for the public sector, then we also need genuine reform. Under capitalism, the public sector has suffered from an excess of bureaucratisation and, in certain areas, a stifling atmosphere which crushes initiative and creativity from staff. This problem will not be solved by importing private sector practices because, contrary to some myths, bureaucratisation also occurs in the private sector. As Max Weber, the classic writer on bureaucracy once noted: 'The very large modern capitalist enterprises are themselves unequalled models of bureaucratic organisation.'[28] Bureaucracy arises when a hierarchy exercises command through its control over knowledge and, if anything, corporate methods have only increased this method of rule in the public sector.

Genuine reform of the Irish public sector, in a society that is moving towards socialism, means expelling this corporate ethos and reducing the layers of management which have created excessive paper work. Reform measures might include:

- **A maximum salary of €100,000.** The salaries of all those who earn more than €150,000 should be cut immediately and, over a period, we should move to a maximum salary of, probably, €100,000. We should recruit people into leading positions who have a real commitment to the public sector and develop a value system that is motivated by an ethos of serving people.

- **End the practice of managerial 'performance bonuses'.** These bonus payments come from the corporate sector and are open to manipulation. Is performance in the HSE, for example, defined by artificial targets or by a genuine rise in the well-being of patients? If there is improved 'performance', it is hardly the work of one individual.

- **Abolish spending on external consultants.** The neoliberals tried to re-shape the public sector by using consultancy firms, such as IBM, who were supposed to have a special organisational expertise. Yet, the evidence suggests that their activities are costly and wasteful. The Personnel, Payroll and Related System (PPARS) in the HSE, for example, was a human resource management and payroll information system. It was supposed to offer better financial management but it ended up costing €131 million before being finally scrapped. The different sets of consultants hired to offer 'project advice' on PPARS included Deloitte and Touche, Hay Market Consultants, ReedSmith Healthcare and IBM. None of them challenged the continuation of the project because of rising costs and, for that reason alone, these consultants should be banished from the public sector forever.

- **Abolish the use of external public relations firms.** This is another practice which was imported from the corporate world. Expensive, glossy and information-poor publications are produced by many state agencies and commissioned from private PR firms. The absurdity was shown when FÁS paid €91,000 to the PR firm Murray Consultants for advice on how to handle a controversy that had arisen from a Dáil Committee investigation into FÁS's waste of money.[29]

- **Cut licensing fees to Microsoft – move to open source software.** A number of German states are increasingly using open source software to avoid paying Microsoft's exorbitant fees. If the Irish public sector adopted open source software, or simply refused to pay Microsoft's tariffs, it would eventually save a vast fortune.

- **Eliminate tendering for outside contractors by doing work in-house.** This is another costly measure foisted on the public sector, often by the neoliberal measures enshrined in EU treaties. The philosophy was to replicate market conditions, and force groups like council employees to 'compete' for their own work against outside contractors. Private firms, however, learn to cut corners and write tenders in ways which reduce the quality of services. The whole procedure costs vast sums in paper work and needlessly duplicates existing capacity.

These measures show how costs can be cut if we challenge the corporate culture imposed on the public sector. But how can the creative energies of its staff be unleashed? Neoliberals assume that public sector staff are themselves the problem – because they are unionised and feel able to assert their rights. Hence the bizarre charge of public sector privilege which emanates from a private media, owned by tax fugitives who do not pay for its upkeep. Linking efficiency in the public sector to a worsening of conditions for staff is inherently counterproductive. You cannot bash public sector workers, and then expect to find high morale among service providers.

We, therefore, make the opposite assumption. Nurses, teachers, firefighters, social workers, council gardeners or maintenance staff have much to offer but are currently oppressed by a culture of managerialism. Giving staff a real opportunity to make decisions on how to run a better public service will benefit everyone as long as it is not used as a fake tool to cut staff numbers or increase workloads. This means a break from the spurious forms of

consultation, often staged by external consultants, where outcomes are decided in advance and where management is merely
'scoping' to find potential sources of opposition.

A number of measures would help here. In a socialist society,
there would be monthly meetings organised, on a non-
hierarchical basis, where staff are allowed to propose changes in
the organisation of the service. Instead of managers chairing staff
meetings, and droning on to assert their authority, chairing could
be rotated, and an open agenda set. Management should be held
accountable to these meetings for their actions.

Union representatives should also be given seats on co-
ordinating bodies which oversee state agencies. During the neoliberal years, these were stuffed full of corporate representatives,
as the example of the HSE illustrates. The current ten-person
board of the HSE includes Willie O'Reilly, the CEO of Today FM;
two bankers, Pat Farrell, the chief executive of the Irish Banking
Federation and Donal de Buitleir, a General Manager, Office of
the Chief Executive, AIB Group; Eugene McCabe, a partner in the
solicitors firm Arthur Cox and a council member of the Dublin
Chamber of Commerce. The chair is Liam Downey, a former chief
executive of Becton Dickson, a medical technology company and a
one time member of the National Executive of IBEC. A more un-
representative sample of Irish society could barely be imagined.
Would a revamped HSE be in a worse state if its board was comprised of trade union representatives as well as representatives of
the poor and the underprivileged?

To reverse the absurdity of the neoliberal years, a change in
language might also be encouraged. People who attend hospitals
or universities are not 'customers' or even 'clients'. They are not
walking wallets to be pounced on for cash. They are, and should
be known as, 'patients' and 'students' who have social rights that
are valued.

Step #6: Build a real knowledge society that expands the intellectual capacity of all

The government claims that the long-term answer to the collapse of the Celtic Tiger lies in creating a knowledge economy, or a 'smart economy', which is based on innovation. The concepts are vague, and are drawn from development theory, but the desire among the population for a more scientific culture is real.

However, the current state strategy relies on 'incentivising' elites, rather than laying a real foundation for the advancement of science. It looks for shortcuts by trying to attract international 'superstar' academics to lead research teams which are staffed with researchers who are kept on roll-over contracts. Much of the research is tailor-made to the immediate needs of corporations. The government has also failed to invest in proper educational equipment for the young during the boom years of the Celtic Tiger. To counteract this short-term strategy, the following measures are required to upskill the population.

- **Reform and expand FÁS to re-skill redundant workers.** FÁS is an example of a state agency with a dedicated staff but with an appalling management structure. The political elite and small private business groupings saw it as a soft touch for junkets and inflated contracts.[30] The management structure should be totally cleaned out and the agency should concentrate on its real purpose, training and re-skilling workers. Redundant workers should be paid an agreed rate while taking up these courses for a limited period.

- **All third level institutions should ensure that at least 25 per cent of their intake is from mature students.** Universities need to be re-organised to end elitist forms of governance and to open them to representatives of the people, while still guaranteeing intellectual freedom. They need to reach out to mature students, as only 13 per cent of college entrants come from this category at present.[31] The National Plan for Equity of Access to Higher Education has set a target of a 20 per cent intake for full-time entrants from 2013, and 27 per cent for all (full-time and part-time) by the same date.[32] These are progressive targets but need to be brought forward and expanded. All universities should be forced to comply with them and adequate resources should also be provided for access courses to facilitate this change. There should be proper long-term investment in community-based adult education programmes.

- **Abolish fees for part-time or night students – do not bring back fees for day students.** The participation level of students from manual working class backgrounds and, particularly, from skilled working class backgrounds has increased since fees were abolished. Over 50 per cent of the children of skilled workers and 30 per cent of those of semi-skilled workers, now attend higher education.[33] However, a PAYE worker who wants to take a college course at night still has to pay fees, even though the course may be exactly the same as that which is offered to daytime students.

- **Introduce a Return to Education credit.** Workers should be allowed to build up credits to gain time off to access colleges. That would offer a real second chance at education.

- **Invest in laboratories in schools.** The quality of Irish education is high but, too often, it can be based on rote learning because of examination pressures. School laboratories should be fully equipped and employ laboratory attendants to encourage a practice of experimentation.

- **Create a full-time cohort of scientific researchers in the third level institution.** You cannot build a twenty-first century knowledge economy on nineteenth century forms of casual labour. Each research institute needs a core of full-time researchers who build up skills and capacities.

- **Abolish rules of intellectual property which impede the progress of science.** These give ownership of knowledge to individuals who seek fees for its use. According to one study, only

14 per cent of US experimental biologists are now willing to talk openly about their current research.[34] Science is impeded when knowledge is privatised and barriers are created against pooling research insights.

Step #7: A state guarantee of the right to work

During the last great depression in the 1930s, Fianna Fáil boldly asserted that the state had a duty to its citizens to guarantee a right to work. They issued a leaflet to counter a statement from a Cumman na nGaedheal Minister for Industry and Commerce, P.J. McGilligan, who said, 'It is not the function of the Dáil to provide work and the sooner this is realised the better ... people may have to die in this country from starvation' with one from Eamon de Valera where he stated that, 'I hope it is the primary duty of a modern state to ensure that every man who is able and willing to work will have work, so that he may earn his daily bread'.[35]

As the spectre of mass unemployment returns, it is ironic that the rhetoric of a conservative republican politician of the 1920s is a great deal more progressive than anything offered by mainstream political leaders today. Or, at least, it would be if it was shorn of its sexist references. Society has, indeed, a duty to share out work, and to ensure that those who want work can find it, and the measures to ensure that include:

- **A reduction in the working week to 35 hours to create jobs.** In 2000, the French government passed a law to reduce the working week to 35 hours, without loss of pay. The measure was fiercely resisted by employers and they eventually over-turned it when the current Prime Minister, Sarkozy, came to power. But one study showed that this mandatory measure, and its voluntary predecessor, had created 285,000 jobs in five years and contributed to a drop in the rate of unemployment.[36]

- **No business declaring profit should be allowed to declare redundancy during the current economic crisis.** The political establishment talk about 'sharing the pain' but there is little sharing when profits rise and workers lose jobs. Workers who occupy their workplaces to save jobs should be fully supported. If it is permissible to interfere in the market to rescue banks, then the same applies to those who occupy workplaces to save jobs, such as occurred in Waterford Crystal, and Visteon in Belfast.

- **Corporations that seek to move elsewhere to benefit from cheaper labour costs should be required to pay back state grants and tax subsidies.** Dell received €55 million in grants for its Limerick plant, so why should it be let walk away without re-paying it? Special claw-backs should also be introduced on depreciation allowances, on tax write-offs for past losses, and on fees earned from patents in software and pharmaceuticals. Funds gained should be used to support alternative forms of employment for those declared redundant.

- **Develop a proper social economy that values work labelled as unproductive because it does not generate profit.** A social economy could employ thousands on care work, on developing community activities, on ending the isolation of the elderly. In the immediate term, the cuts in the Community Employment Schemes should be reversed, as these schemes perform valuable services and help generate a real community spirit.

Step #8: Protect pensions – create a guaranteed income for the elderly

The current crash has set off a pension time bomb under Irish society because employers forced workers into defined contribution schemes. A disproportionate share of Irish-managed pension funds has been invested in the Irish stock exchange – which has fallen faster and more dramatically than elsewhere.

- **Increase the social welfare pension to at least 50 per cent of the average industrial wage.** The social welfare pension accounts for 60 per cent of pensioners' total income and 80 per cent of the income of the poorest three-fifths.[37] The increased costs could be partially offset by reducing tax relief on the pensions of those who earn more than €100,000. A small group of people earning over €250,000 annually shared a staggering €121 million in tax relief in 2005. (The 2009 Budget cut this earning ceiling to €150,000 a year).[38]

- **Turn the social welfare pension into a guaranteed income for over-65s**. There are many complications arising from incomplete records and means tests, and women are particularly disadvantaged as they often provide care for children and elderly relatives. Women who worked in the civil service until 1973 were forced to leave work and were not entitled to a pension in their own right. The social welfare pensions should, therefore, be universalised, transforming them into a guaranteed income that is available for all long-term residents who reach 65.

- **Require employers to make a mandatory contribution to an employee pension fund.** Currently, employers need only to facilitate a worker's access to a private pension fund. In Norway, however, they are legally obliged to make a minimum 2 per cent contribution each year. There is no reason why it could not be considerably higher in a different society.

- **Ban pension investment in hedge funds and abolish fees charged by pension fund managers.** Nothing illustrates the absurdity of modern capitalism more than the way the savings of working people have been squandered by the pension industry. Pensions were recklessly invested in speculation to achieve ever higher returns for fund managers. There should be a European-wide ban on this activity and only a fractional charge to cover administration. A special state bond should be established to receive pension investment and to repay future generations. The National Pension Reserve Fund should withdraw from speculative activity and contribute, instead, to long-term state investment programmes.

Step #9: Shift from light regulation to heavy regulation

The policy of light regulation helped make the crash deeper in Ireland than elsewhere. One of the major public advocates of this approach was none other than Sean Fitzpatrick, formerly of Anglo Irish Bank. He was one of the key figures who successfully campaigned against the Companies (Audit and Accountancy) Act of 2003 which required company directors to issue annual compliance statements about their internal controls and tax law. According to Fitzpatrick, 'we need to legislate to the necessary minimum, supplemented by codes of corporate governance and good business practice'.[39] In other words, he advocated a high degree of self-regulation. This 'light touch' was administered by friendly regulatory authorities who were stuffed full of corporate advisors or by state officials who aspired to become corporate executives on retirement.

To change this, we should:

- **Give a majority representation on all regulatory agencies to voluntary organisations from civil society**, including trade unions, user bodies, local communities and representatives of the poor. This would give these agencies more teeth and produce a better over-sight role.

- **Ban anyone serving on these bodies from participating in the organisations they regulate for at least five years after retirement**. This would reduce any incentive to go soft in the hope of procuring a well paid job afterwards.

- **Introduce a whistle blower's charter to protect workers who reveal the corporate crimes and misdemeanours of their employers**. Currently, many organisations, including the HSE, attempt to limit the freedom of speech of their employees.

- **Expand the number of inspectors in agencies such as the Health and Safety Authority and the Labour Inspectorate, and create an inspectorate to oversee landlords**. Currently, inspection of workplaces for health and safety standards or

breaches in labour law, is comparatively rare. There is virtually no overseeing of private rented accommodation, whereas,
in a fairer society, we would value high quality standards.

- **Introduce large-scale random audits of companies to ensure
they are compliant with the laws of the country.** At present,
the Revenue Commissioners only carry out about 400 random
audits and 14,000 target audits a year. Yet, these raised €687
million in 2007. Why not increase the number of random audits?

All of the proposals outlined in this chapter are made to advance a practical social agenda for change. They infringe on the
logic of the for-profit economy because adherence to that framework offers no longer-term solution. Achieving this agenda
would require a degree of popular mobilisation that challenges
the power of the wealthy. In the course of such mobilisation, more
proposals for change will emerge and will, undoubtedly, produce
even more resistance from privileged interests. This raises the
question of just how practical are such proposals? Is it really possible to foresee a society where these measures are carried out? In
the next chapter we will discuss this issue.

Endnotes

---

[1] 'Erin Go Broke', *New York Times*, 19 April 2009.

[2] 'Dempsey accuses wrong doers at Anglo of economic treason', *Irish
Times*, 24 February 2009.

[3] Copy of S&P report on http://ftalphaville.ft.com/blog/2009/03/30/54198/
sp-strips-ireland-of-its-triple-a-rating/?source=rss.

[4] IMF Companion Paper: *The State of Public Finances – Outlook and Medium Term Policies after 2008 Crash*, 6 March 2009, p. 17.

[5] Department of Finance, *Macroeconomic and fiscal framework 2009-2013*,
pp. 10-12.

[6] ' See J. Stiglitz, 'Let Bad Banks Fail', *Daily Telegraph*, 2 February 2009; P.
Romer, 'Let's Start Brand New Banks', *Wall Street Journal*, 6 February

2009; W. Buiter, 'The Good bank Solution' http://blogs.ft.com/ maverecon/ 2009/01/the-good-bank-solution/.

[7] 'Stop Bailing out bad banks and build a good one', *Irish Times,* 24 March 2009.

[8] 'Fairer way to ease the crisis', *Irish Times,* 3 April 2009.

[9] 'Legal Advisor for bank bail out was also acting for BOI', *Sunday Tribune,* 22 February 2009.

[10] 'Anglo Books are a who's who of the Celtic Tiger', *Sunday Independent,* 26 December 2008.

[11] 'Nationalised banks would find it harder to get funds', *Irish Times,* 25 April 2009.

[12] 'Nationalising the banks is the best option', *Irish Times,* 17 April 2009.

[13] A. Barrett, I. Kearney, J. Goggin, *ESRI Quarterly Commentary Spring 2009* (Dublin: ESRI, 2009), p. 1.

[14] 'Japan's Big Works Stimulus is lesson', *New York Times,* 5 February 2009.

[15] SEI report, *Energy Consumption and CO 2 Emissions in the Residential Sector 1990–2004* (Dublin: SEI, 2005).

[16] Press Release, ' RESS describe EUR 100 million insulation programme 'as a drop in the ocean', 9 February 2009.

[17] Press Release: 'Government announces new national insulation programme', http://www.greenparty.ie/en/news/latest_news/govt_ announces_ new_national_insulation_programme.

[18] 'HSE must replace half of long stay nursing home beds to meet standards' *Irish Examiner* 8 April 2009.

[19] Department of Health, *Primary care: A New Direction* (Dublin: Department of Health, 2001); M. Wren, *Unhealthy State* (Dublin: New Island, 2003), p. 211.

[20] 'Ireland has 5.4 trillion of oil lying off west coast', *Daily Mirror,* 30 January 2009.

[21] G. Wilpert, 'Venezuela Decrees Nationalization of Last Foreign Controlled Oil Fields', Venezuelaanalysis.com, 27 February 2007.

[22] N. Martinez, *Bolivia Nationalization: Understanding the Process and Gauging the Results* (Washington: Institute for Policy Studies, 2007), p. 2.

[23] 'Revenue data understate contribution of lower and middle income earners', *Irish Times,* 20 March 2009.

[24] Bank of Ireland, *The Wealth of the Nation* (Dublin: Bank of Ireland, 2008), p. 12.

[25] Parliamentary answer to Joan Burton produced in her press release: New Figures show huge sums spent on property based tax relief schemes, 17 November 2008.

[26] Dail Debates, Vol. 665., No 1, 24 September 2008. Reply to written question 343.

[27] Comptroller and Auditor General, *The Grouped Schools Pilot Partnership Project* (Dublin: Government Publications, 2004), p. 11.

[28] M. Weber, *Economy and Society Volume 2* (Berkeley: University of California Press, 1978), p. 974.

[29] 'Fas Paid €91,000 for PR advice', *Sunday Tribune,* 19 April 2009.

[30] Dáil Eireann, Committee of Public Accounts, *Fourth Interim Report on Special Report 10 of the Comptroller and Auditor General and Fas 2007 Accounts,* February 2009, PRN A9/0015.

[31] HEA, *National Plan for Equity Access to Higher Education 2008-2013* (Dublin: HEA 2008), p. 27.

[32] Ibid pp 60-61.

[33] Ibid p 25

[34] J.P. Walsh and W. Hong, 'Secrecy Increasing in Step with Competition', *Nature* no. 422 (24 April 2003) pp. 801-2.

[35] Sean McEntee Papers, P 67/346, UCD Archives.

[36] 'The French miracle: A Shorter working week, more jobs and men doing the ironing, '*The Independent,* 19 June 2001.

[37] TASC, *Making Pensions works for People* (Dublin TASC, 2008) p. 13.

[38] Ibid, p. 9.

[39] 'Bill will stifle business – Banker', *Irish Times,* 1 May 2003.

6

PEOPLE POWER

JAMES CONNOLLY IS ONE OF THE ICONS of Irish society, with a major hospital and a train station named after him. Each year, a small number of trade unionists from SIPTU gather to lay a wreath at his grave on the date of his execution, 12 May 1916. Yet, this revered figure was once considered a dangerous radical, who often faced the question: Were his ideas practical? His reply was interesting:

> In the phraseology of politics, a party too indifferent to the sorrow and sufferings of humanity to raise its voice in protest, is a moderate, practical party; whilst a party totally indifferent to the personality of leaders, but hot with enthusiasm on every question affecting the well-being of the toiling masses, is an extreme, a dangerous party.

> Moral – Don't be 'practical' in politics. To be practical in that sense means that you have schooled yourself to think along the lines, and in the grooves those who rob you would desire you to think.[1]

Modern mainstream politics has been reduced to choices which are limited by parameters set by a for-profit economy. Instead of asking what does society need, the main political question becomes, what is feasible within current economic constraints? This is the fundamental basis for a political consensus that stretches across the mainstream parties. There are set-piece battles on the floor of Dáil Éireann and parties fight elections with great gusto but there is also a shared agenda. Fine Gael may challenge Fianna Fáil's 'litany of failure', and propose public sector cuts rather than tax rises, but both agree that society at large must bear the cost of the current economic crisis. Labour may verbally decry the injustice of levies on PAYE workers but opposes strikes to resist a pension levy. Opposition, it is implied, has to be left to experienced politicians who will guide it through safe channels. With crunch issues, such as the Lisbon Treaty, the main parties unite in economic blackmail: if the population doesn't recognise the error of its ways and vote Yes, there will be further economic ruin.

Clearly, from this perspective, the proposals outlined in the last chapter are 'impractical'. They challenge the limits of a for-profit economy and assert that the wealthy must pay for an economic crisis that they created. The proposals demand that society puts the interests of the poor and vulnerable before that of the bankers. Instead of a rhetoric about 'sharing the pain', they boldly assert that low and middle income groups not be targeted. The proposals are entirely workable or 'practical', but are totally unacceptable to the wealthy elite.

However, every major reform in human society has involved a clash between the logic of what people need and the limits set by their society. Apartheid would still exist in South Africa, women would still be deprived of the vote and trade unions would still be semi-clandestine organisations, if people had not revolted. A few people rebel for a vision of a better world; others rebel because of disgruntlement with aspects of their lives. However, the most serious revolts occur when, to paraphrase Lenin, rulers can no longer rule in the old way and the mass of people refuse what they are offered. In other words, revolts do not spring from the fiery words of agitators or the visionary speeches of prophets – they arise from the deep contradictions within a society.

There is often an interesting dynamic between revolts and economic downturn. Contrary to economic determinist thinking, people do not automatically revolt when they see their world crashing around them because poverty and hunger can be great pacifiers as they force people back onto the most elementary modes of survival. But the sudden collapse or bankruptcy of the old order, as is revealed at present, can also tear legitimacy away from elites. Confidence in their actions declines and leaders, who were once thought to have Teflon-like qualities, appear as buffoons. The aura of leadership and gravitas slips from their shoulders. Splits also develop within the tight networks that govern society and political adventurers arise to court popularity. But how masses of people respond to such crises is never determined in advance.

Broadly, the pattern is one of conflicting emotions. On one hand, a great fear sweeps the country as people worry about their jobs and the welfare of their families. From this fear arises an acceptance of measures that were inconceivable in different periods. No one, for example, ever envisaged that Irish workers would accept wage cuts in the twenty-first century. But alongside the fear, there is also a deep anger which can turn to rage. Notwithstanding what the political establishment say, people know they are paying for the economic crimes of the bankers. They know that behind the bankers stand the developers and a rich layer of Irish society, who have the political establishment at their beck and call. And many want to protest and even stage a revolution.

Two scenarios from the last great depression of the 1930s have some relevance to modern-day Ireland.

After the Wall Street crash of 1929, the US economy shrank by 10 per cent, then 16 per cent in 1932 and 30 per cent in 1933.[2] The labour movement entered the depression in a weak state, having lost one million members during the 1920s while the employers used the crisis to impose further defeats and wage cuts. They refused to bargain with unions and pushed union organisers out of factories. Naturally, this produced a great wave of opposition, as many joined hunger demonstrations and, in response, employers sometimes played the race card to divide workers. In the deep South, for example, anti-union leaflets appeared with the headline, 'Would you belong to a union which opposes white supremacy'.[3] Broadly, in this early period, workers suffered many defeats but alongside the defeats grew a deep politicisation and a strong anti-capitalist sentiment.

Then, in 1934, the tide turned dramatically. There were three very militant struggles in Toledo, San Francisco, and, most spectacularly, in Minneapolis, where pitched battles were fought between mass flying pickets and the police.[4] Union victories in these struggles paved the way for a campaign of mass unionisation that began with the formation of the Congress of Industrial Organisations. This revolt from below also deeply affected the reform agenda of the Roosevelt Presidency. He had begun to make concessions to workers with his first National Recovery Act in 1933, but as the concessions mounted, the so called progressive wing of the business establishment began to desert Roosevelt. As Mike Davis put it, 'this mass desertion of business from the administration in 1935 drove a reluctant Roosevelt temporarily into the hands of the CIO insurgents'[5] Pressure from below then brought about a further radicalisation of Roosevelt's New Deal package, with the National Labour Relations Act, for example, making it illegal for employers to refuse to bargain with unions.

What appeared thoroughly 'impractical' at the start of a depression became the common sense of the era because of huge popular pressure. Fear subsided and as it was replaced by anger, the accumulated grievances and bitterness broke through. The success of the US labour movement in the 1930s was, of course, double-edged, forcing concessions from Roosevelt but also creating new openings for union leaders to be co-opted into the political structures. More crucially, the New Deal did not solve the crisis but the alliance forged between the unions and Roosevelt produced a reorganisation of capitalism. In brief, the system was effectively saved from itself, unfortunately, as the cost was a more militarised society that has stayed with us to this day.

The other scenario of the 1930s is much better known. The 1929 crash in Germany was equally steep, and in its wake there was also a change of the political landscape. The Nazi vote jumped from just over three-quarters of a million in 1928 to six million in 1929 and they moved from being the ninth largest party to the second.[6] Fascism, unlike conventional right wing politics, also involved a degree of popular mobilisation. But through its physical control of the streets, it tried to turn its supporters into supermen so that they could beat down Jews, migrants and other 'deviants'. Fascism was a counter-revolutionary movement that grew out of the rage of middle layers whose lives were destroyed by the crisis.

These two cameos encapsulate tendencies that emerge in a great economic crisis. History hardly repeats itself, and they are not offered as templates for the future. They merely illustrate that, when people's lives are ruptured, they can either band together collectively or, in despair, they can look for scapegoats to stamp on. A shift to the left arises from a strong sense of solidarity and a knowledge that fighting back is the only way to stop being trampled on. The first stirrings of revolt often bring defeats, but if they do not lead to a passive fatalism, bitter lessons are learnt for future struggles. A shift to the right grows from a desperate clinging to the old mottos of a discredited system. It springs from resentment that the state is not 'looking after its own' and that migrants are 'stealing' the jobs and welfare of the natives. Both tendencies are already becoming evident in Ireland's great depression. Which tendency become uppermost is dependent on a host of political factors.

MOBILISATION

When writing about eighteenth century Britain, the historian E.P. Thompson went to great lengths to disabuse readers of a notion that crowds who rioted and protested were a 'mob'. This perspective ran counter to a traditional historiography which saw such crowds as merely inflamed by emotion. Thompson, however, used the concept of a 'moral economy' to indicate how people used traditional norms and customs to rationalise and legitimate their actions.[7] People built up their own sense of fairness and social obligations, which eventually clashed with the ambitions of their economic masters. These norms developed in times of social peace when deference and acceptance of the existing social order seemed universal. When this 'moral economy' is challenged, people, who have slotted into the quiet grooves of life, rebel.

Something similar is happening in Ireland. The first great mobilisation about the current economic crisis came from an unexpected quarter. In October 2008, the Fianna Fáil–Green government introduced an emergency budget which attacked both the elderly and the young. Over-70 year-olds were originally granted free medical treatment as a result of an electoral manoeuvre by politicians to secure their votes, yet this concession soon entered the moral economy of the population at large. It was seen as a social right which the elderly had won through their past contributions to Irish society. The Fianna Fáil–Green government, however, withdrew the medical cards and launched an attack on the very idea of universal benefits, insisting on means-testing for medical care.

The result was one of the most spectacular protests ever seen. Starting with an assembly in a church, a social movement emerged that drew on networks created by 'active retirement' groups. Soon, 15,000 people marched on the parliament, making full use of the free travel scheme, another 'gift' of an opportunist politician, to ride the trains to Dublin. Handwritten placards proclaimed, 'Our Patriotic Duty: Revolution'; 'Rob the pensioners to bail out the bankers'; 'Why don't you shoot us now?' Government ministers, who thought they would receive some deference from the elderly when they expressed their 'understanding and sorrow', were booed off the stage. Within days, the government was forced to retreat, making apologies for its 'insensitivity'.

Soon after the pensioners revolted, it was the turn of parents of younger children and teenagers. The desire for education, even if only as a means to social advancement, is deeply embedded in Irish society. Yet the Fianna Fáil–Green government introduced savage cutbacks in school funding and this, too, provoked a wave of protest. In a series of huge mobilisations, teachers joined with parents on a number of larger marches. This time, the government fared somewhat better because the teachers' union leaders did not show the same militancy as the elderly. Nevertheless, the government was forced to make some small concessions.

While these struggles were underway, the Waterford Crystal workers offered an even more inspiring example of resistance. In a free market society, workers are supposed to meekly accept their lot and allow themselves to be discarded like disposable hankies when they are no longer profitable. The glass workers, however, refused to accept this logic and occupied their plant; more than 2,000 people came out in bitter weather to show their solidarity. Many asked the elegantly simple question: If they can save the bankers, why not the workers? Their struggle eventualy inspired workers in Visteon in Belfast to also occupy their plant, and force the gigantic Ford motor company to pay them a huge redundancy settlement.

The question remains: If there was such a willingness to fight, why has it not been carried through to outright rebellion?

Even while these battles were being fought, the Irish ruling class regrouped. The commentariat of the conservative media lambasted the government for its weakness and urged 'decisive' leadership. Stephen Colllins, the political correspondant of the *Irish Times*, for example, denounced the 'hysterical' reaction to the October budget and urged Brian Cowen to 'go for broke' with a programme of tax hikes and cutbacks.[8] Soon the new agenda of targeting public sector workers came into full view as a 'pension levy' was imposed as a blatant ploy to circumvent legal obstacles to a wage cut. Before embarking on this course, the government took the precaution of embroiling the union leaders in discussions on 'stabilising the finances', and then, at the very last moment, landed the proposal for a pension levy on them. Some thought the move was choreographed to get the unpalatable issue of wage cuts out of the way so that social partnership discussions could resume at a later stage.

The reaction of the grassroots union members was one of huge anger. On 21 February 2009, over 120,000 people came out on the streets of Dublin, and many took up the call raised by the left for a one-day national strike. The response from the union leaders was, however, ambiguous and cowardly. Instead of telling the government that workers would not pay for the crisis, they talked about a 'fairer sharing of the pain'. They hired a Swedish social democrat as a consultant to develop a ten point plan which demanded greater tax concessions from the rich, but failed to demand the full withdrawal of the levy. Like old singers who could not learn new tunes, they imagined that the game of threatening action and then calling it off to enter partnership talks was still in play. They hoped that, after the display of strength on the 21st of February, the government would invite them back into a 'national consensus' to solve the problem of the Irish economy. So, they called a ballot for a national strike on March 30th, but, behind the scenes, maintained close contacts with the government in the hope that social partnership could be restored.

When the votes came through, there was an overwhelming vote for strike action. Much was made of the failure of IMPACT to gain a two-thirds majority for strike sanction but, in fact, 65 per cent of members voted for a strike even though its leadership never conveyed the slightest determination to fight. The ICTU leaders, however, called off the national strike, without consulting their members, in order to hold even more talks with the government. Few commentators who expressed support for 'democratic forms of government' showed any concern for this blatant disregard for democracy. The talks were a bit like two generals agreeing to have a cup of tea while one slaughtered the other's soldiers.

It was a disastrous move that arose from a fundamental misunderstanding of union leaders' own role in society. Flattered by their apparent access to the corridors of power and rewarded with posts on the boards of agencies such as FÁS, they imagined that they might be treated as equal partners in a 'social solidarity pact'. They forgot, or possibly never imagined, that the state regards them only as labour brokers – useful for imposing discipline on their members but marginal when other methods can be employed. During the boom times, social partnership was used to keep wage increases down and to win agreement for neoliberal policies that were wrapped in the vacuous language of 'social inclusion', but when the crash occurred, the employers' and the government's agenda changed. Their solution lay in outright wage cuts to restore 'competetiveness' and, while the union leaders might be consulted, the flattery was over if they did not assent.

When struggles occur over such enormous issues, the question of leadership becomes paramount. After being initially thrown off course by popular mobilisation, the government re-grouped and lashed out in an even more determined fashion. By contrast - fear, timidity and the sheer incompetance of the union leaders led to a great wave of demoralisation. Many, who once cheered the elderly in defeating the government, began to ask, 'is there nothing we can do?' From this fatalism and defeatism grew a wider acceptance of the dominant consensus as fear began to predominate over anger. A deep distrust also developed about a union leadership that showed such an unwillingess to fight.

This shift in the balance between fear and anger is temporary and highly volatile. In every great crisis where people want to resist, they do not initially have the tools to do so. Old understandings of the world clash with the new experience of a brutal assult on living standards. In the past, it was good enough to 'sit back' and allow the unions to operate like a social insurance policy. Now, however, workers, both blue collar and white collar, private sector and public sector, are confronted with constant demands to cover for redundant workers, to tear up old agreements in the interest of 'competitiveness', to accept more wage cuts. Outside the workplaces, an already inadequate health service is being torn to shreds and elemenary social infrastructure, whether it is a drug rehabilitation programme or support mechanisms for the disabled, is being ruptured. The choice of fighting back or watching every gain of the past decade being trampelled on is becoming more poignant than ever.

ALTERNATIVES

Three major developments need to occur if society is to be rescued from the immense hardship which the government and the elites want to load on to it.

Grassroots organisations need to develop that are capable of mobilising large numbers of people – because the legacy of social partnership has been a wholescale co-option of the voices of opposition. Too many organisations have seen their representatives go to government buildings and come back talking the language of moderation and obedience. A technique of 'blowing off steam' has become the fine art of Irish politics. At large-scale meetings, people are perfectly free to ventilate their anger, usually with great eloquence, until the dead hand of moderation comes down to close off protest. Defeatism and fatalism have become the stock and trade of every 'practical' union leader or community representative.

To combat this, new forms of grassroots organisation need to develop. Workers should take back control of their unions from paid officials who do not own the organisation. If necessary, they should elect new shop stewards and representatives who do not aspire to get close to their managers or to use the position to gain promotion. Instead of 'the union' being an external body that bureaucratically processes each issue to the Labour Relations Commission, it needs to become a living organisation based on workplace solidarity. Regular mass meetings should be held where the voices of members are not drowned out by endless speeches from officials who are more interested in displaying their verbal dexterity. There should be no fear of debate or voting on which tactics best advance the interests of the union. A lesson might usefully be learnt from Polish workers when they set up the free, independent trade union, Solidarnosc: Never let your representatives talk in secret to your opponents – always make them report back on negotiations. This form of grassroots trade unionism is the only one that is capable of dealing with the current onslaught. In almost every workplace, workers are being asked, for example, to take on extra work. Many want to refuse or, at least, to know what existing workloads must be discarded before they take on other work duties. Resistance can only develop through a renewal of trade union organisation at the workplace.

Workplace organisation will also expand quicker if national union leaderships are challenged. Many workers want co-ordinated action that gives confidence, rather than having to fight alone, and would like to see national French-style stoppages. But if unions are led by people who are paid two or three times the salaries of their membership, there are significant problems. If leadership is not renewed through the election of new fighters who come from the grassroots, it stagnates. Current union leaders have become far too close to the political establishment and are incapable of leading any serious fight. Instead, they dovetail the outlook of the Labour Party, as is evident in the way they heeded Eamon Gilmore's advice not to take industrial action on March 30th. This needs to be changed through open electoral contests or through deeper, structural changes.

Grassroots organisation is not confined to the unions. Although largely unnoticed by the conventional media, a strong sentiment exists in Ireland for a politics of 'people power'. Local community organisations can spring to life quickly and can bring hundreds onto the streets to oppose planning decisions or bin charges. Groups like Shell to Sea have displayed an extraordinary resilience in the face of jailings and police violence to sustain a long struggle against one of the largest corporations in the world. However, once again, a similar tension exists within community organisation as well as the unions. Alongside displays of militancy, there are countervailing tendencies which stress a form of professionalism which is opposed to mass activity. This 'leave it to the expert' approach invites people to look to legal specialists or local councillors to 'make representations' on their behalf.

If water charges are introduced – as appears likely – a new round of struggle will open up in communities which can only be fought through resistance and defiance as this is how they were defeated in the past. In 1994, water charges were introduced on the spurious grounds of providing local authorities with additional revenue, but they were met with an open rebellion in working class areas. People, quite simply, refused to pay and, where council officials turned off water, it was turned back on again unofficially. Those involved were denounced as 'water bandits' by the *Evening Herald* but nothing could break the campaign .When those who refused to pay were brought before the courts, crowds of up to 500 gathered outside. Mass action was combined with electoral intervention when Joe Higgins won a seat in the Dáil. The experience showed that grassroots organisation was the key to victory.

The second requirement for opposing social suffering in the current crisis is the emergence of a radical left.

The experience in other countries shows that a re-composition of left politics is underway, even before the curent global crash. In Germany, a new political party, Die Linke, has developed through a split in the Social Democratic Party. It has brought together many varied elements on the left and now faces great internal debate on whether or not it should join a government in capitalist society. In France, the New Anti-Capitalist party has been founded on a more explicitly revolutionary agenda and its spokesperson, Olivier Besancenot, has won huge popularity. The different models reflect differing levels of social conflict but the experiences are relevant to Ireland.

The left in Ireland is currently dominated by Labour and Sinn Féin, but neither have shown the capacity or the interest in promoting radical forms of people power. Labour has signalled a modest turn to the left by differentiating itself from Fine Gael and actively condemning the bail out of the banks. However, its shift is deeply contradictory. The party holds to the idea of a national consensus to solve Ireland's economic woes. Its ultimate aim is to shore up its electoral base by tacking left and then entering a coalition government with the right. When its representatives are repeatedly asked, would you rule out coalition with Fine Gael, they refuse to.

Sinn Féin is also experiencing a considerable flux. It had the singular misfortune to start its journey to the right just as the economic crisis began. In an unusual move, the party voted for the bank bail out, giving rise to the joke that the IRA's political wing decided to stop taking money out of banks and put in some state money instead. The party's most recent economic policy documents advocate more tax credits for multinational firms who source Irish products, as well as additional state support for Irish capitalists.[9] Like Labour, the party is positioning itself to join a coalition government with the right.

This leaves open a wide space for a political force that provides an alternative to simply managing capitalism. Such a force should base itself on 'people power' movements and seek a change that comes from below. It should not tailor its programme to what is feasible under capitalism but demand what the majority need. It should support workers who strike; it should back resistance to water charges; it should champion unity by opposing racism and sexism. It should commit itself in advance to electing people who will take the average workers' wage and who will rule out any coalition or deals with the right. This alternative has begun to emerge with the People Before Profit Alliance, which brings together activists from diverse backgrounds. The alliance puts a focus on 'people power' as a way to bring change while also contesting local and national elections. It looks set to play a major role in the construction of a radical left.

The third requirement is a revival of socialist politics – which asserts that another economy is possible.

Such an economy could develop if we take the large corporations into public ownership, and re-organise our economy to serve human needs, and not profit. A corporation is a legal entity which allows shareholders to take the fruits of the labour of others. The largest blocks of shares are controlled by a handful of people who add nothing to the production process – they do not work, plan or even help sell what is produced. They merely buy coupons which allow them a share in the exploitation of others. The modern corporation is, therefore, organised around a dictatorship of money, where richest millionaires get several million votes to select a board of directors while middle class shareholders get a handful. The sole purpose of the board of directors is 'shareholder value', or maximising the exploitation of workers. Some money may have to be spent on PR to pretend that there is 'corporate social responsibility' but, in reality, a corporation is really a collective psychopath that does not care about its workforce or about its impact on the environment. Socialism means taking such corporations into public ownership.

A simple example will illustrate. There are ten corporations which control half of all legal drugs which are produced on the planet. Each has about fifteen people on its board of directors, often representing other corporations in an interlocking chain. This means that about 150 people dictate the collective labour of millions of people and the purpose for which they are set to work. Instead of producing drugs for the sickest people, they spend approximately 30 per cent of sales on marketing, to convince healthy people that they may be sick. Between 1975 and 1997, 1,393 new drugs were produced but only sixteen were for tropical illnesses.[10] Socialism means giving redundancy notices to this golden 150 so that the pharmaceutical industry is owned in common, and cheap generic drugs are produced for the sickest and the poorest. In Ireland, the redundancy notices should be handed to the golden 20 executive directors who run the banks.

Contrary to any caricature, this does not involve the seizure of wealth from workers or even middle income groups. There is no need for a socialist society to nationalise restaurants, bicycle shops or design agencies. It need only establish a new legal framework to guarantee workers' rights or limit exploitation in such enterprises. An Irish socialist society need only take control of the banks, the major construction companies, the major manufacturing plants and distribution outlets.

Public ownership of large corporations would make possible a change in the nature of work as modern work processes are based on a sharp division between thinking and doing. A managerial layer, whose first loyalty is to the shareholders, does all the thinking, planning and conception, deciding on what is produced, how products are designed, how work is organised. As capitalism grows older, they expand in numbers and even develop their own strange business-speak, sometimes punctuating sentences with the absurd phrase 'going forward'. By contrast, the mass of workers, whether blue collar or white collar, 'are not paid to think' and have no say about what is produced or how work is organised. A handful of overpaid managers, therefore, function like the priesthood of old – they are all-wise and all-seeing, and, it is assumed, that only they could possible know how to organise.

We should end this absurd fiction, and develop a new system of workers' control of production. Workers should periodically discuss how to run their enterprises. They should be free to discuss better ways to raise productivity without feeling this will lead to job losses. Higher forms of productivity should benefit all, through, for example, cutting the working time, or enabling workers to build up credits to access higher forms of learning. This breakdown of the division between thinking and doing could do away with vast amounts of unproductive, overpaid managers. Undoubtedly, in any large organisation, some people will still need to function as co-ordinators, but these could be elected democratically, or else the function could rotate. Workers' control, rather than managerial dictates, could potentially unleash the creative energies of millions who are now told 'not to think'.

Even if the large corporations were taken into public ownership and workers control of production prevailed, there must still be a mechanism through which the resources of society are allocated for different human needs. Instead of pretending that there is a great machine known as the Market, which we must adore but not interfere with, we need democratic structures to allocate resources, and to plan what will be produced.

Considerable confusion still exists about a planned economy, and it is still associated with the former 'communist' regimes in Eastern Europe. But they had as much resemblance to socialism as the Spanish Inquisition had with the teachings of Jesus Christ. Typically, a handful of people in the Politburo of the Communist Party made decisions on where investment was to be allocated. Their overall aim was to reduce consumption – the share of an economy distributed to workers – and to transfer resources to heavy industry. During the Cold War, investment in the iron and steel industry was intimately connected to the arms industry and planning was driven by the logic of military competition rather than the needs of the mass of people. Output targets for each sector of the economy were, accordingly, decided through bureaucratic commands, but this led to its own internal form of chaos. When the Politburo in Moscow ordered so many tons of raw pig iron to be produced, the local bureaucrats in Minsk or Odessa conformed by either producing inferior quality goods or by manipulating the figures. Without genuine transparency or accountability, the economy relied on fictitious data that made genuine planning impossible. Clearly, this form of planning does not represent a viable alternative to modern capitalism.

Genuine socialist planning requires all economic information to be made available to the public, and this would represent a huge transformation from our present society. Despite hypocritical talk of transparency, modern economies are shrouded in secrecy, as Irish banking demonstrates. The Irish people still do not know exactly how much bad debt the Irish banks have or who controls their large blocks of shares. Even though Anglo Irish Bank is nationalised, people are not told about the assets of the developers who have taken out huge loans from the bank. Democratic planning requires the abolition of such commercial secrecy as there is no need for it in an economy built around co-operation rather than competition.

This outline of a possible alternative economy is sketchy and has a certain utopian quality about it. The practical politician of today will, no doubt, regard it as highly idealistic and impossible. But the same practical politician assumed that modern capitalism was a stable system where the spectre of a 1930s depression had been banished forever. Many still assume that the current economic difficulties are only 'a blip' before a stable normal economy resumes again. The reality, however, is that the recovery of the for-profit system will come at a huge social cost as investment will only revive when wages and social conditions have been driven down as far as they can go. And when it does pick up, there will be a huge overhang of debt which will rule out any social advance for decades to come.

If this is the aging economic system we will live under, we need to make the aspirations for a better world a reality.

Endnotes

[1] J. Connolly, *Workshop Talks* (Cork: Cork Workers Club, 1997), p. 5.

[2] L. Chandler, *America's Greatest Depression, 1929-1941* (New York: Harper Row, 1970), p. 20.

[3] B. Cochran, *Labor and Communism: The Conflict that Shaped American Unions* (Princeton: Princeton University Press, 1977), p. 35.

[4] F. Dobbs, *Teamster Rebellion* (New York: Pathfinder Press, 1972).

[5] M. Davis, *Prisoners of the American Dream* (London: Verso, 1986), p. 63.

[6] A. Bullock, *Hitler: A Study in Tyranny* (Harmondsworth: Penguin, 1990), p. 161.

[7] E. P. Thompson, 'The Moral Economy of the English Crowd in the 18th Century'. *Past & Present*, 50 (1971), pp. 76-136.

[8] 'Cowen has nothing to lose by going for broke in the budget', *Irish Times*, 14 March 2009.

[9] Sinn Féin, *Getting Ireland back to work* (Dublin: Sinn Féin, 2009) pp. 3-4.

[10] P. Trouiller, O. Piero, E. Torreele, J. Orbinski, R. Laing, N. Ford, 'Drug development for neglected diseases: a deficient market and a public heath failure', *The Lancet*, Vol. 359, No. 9324, 22 June 2002, pp. 2188-2194.

INDEX